Destiny at Trichy

Michael Maher &
Julie Marsh

Copyright © 2023 by Buriedshiva Productions
ISBN 978-0-9808370-2-5

Cover design by Michael Maher
Book design by Michael Maher
Cover photo: Julie at Thanjavur's Big Temple

No part of this book may be reproduced in any form or by any electronic or mechanical means including information storage and retrieval systems, without permission in writing from the author. The only exception is by a reviewer, who may quote short excerpts in a review.

Visit the author's Web sites:
michaels-music.buriedshiva.com.au/
youtube.com/user/MichaelM1052
michaelmaher.bandcamp.com/music

Contact: publishing@buriedshiva.com.au

Destiny at Trichy
A Journey of Survival

Contents

Destiny at Trichy 3

Part I 7

  INDIA 7

    The Temples 8

    The Fire 16

    GVN and Hotel Sathyam 22

    GVN Intensive Care Unit (ICU) 26

    GVN ICU Week 2 35

    GVN Medical Ward 60

Part II 101

  AUSTRALIA 101

    Armidale Hospital 102

    Prince of Wales Hospital, Sydney 113

    Return to Armidale Hospital 153

    Return to Prince of Wales Hospital, Sydney 158

    Armidale Hospital for third time 162

  Identity 165

  Epilogue 170

  Afterword (Julie) 174

Part I

INDIA

The Temples

Throughout life, some events inspire us to question the intentions of the universe. Julie and I had both been seeking something unique from this journey through India. We knew it may be our final and longest adventure here, travelling to many new places within the country that over years we had come to know so well.

India often delivers the unexpected; yet, hoping for experiences which would alter our lives towards a more purposeful last phase, we couldn't foresee that those encounters may ultimately be devastating. We couldn't envisage that what transpired may become a positive force for change through the crucible of fire – the gift of Saturn, one of the most revered of deities in the Hindu pantheon: he who forces us beyond our limits.

What began one warm Spring evening in South India, extending into the following months and persisting long after our return to Australia, cast us into a whirlwind of confusion, fear and amazement. Now, with hindsight of some years, while the difficulties continue, I can say the entire saga is about *trust*.

Friday, January 24

I have loved India from a young age, and Julie being a historian of South Asia, together we often revisit, always wanting to absorb more, keenly perceptive of its social, cultural, political changes. Nearing the end of this journey, after moving for five months through North and South India, we'd scheduled a visit to one last area of historic temples, Chola Nadu (in Tamil Nadu), before our final weeks in the pleasing familiarity of Fort Cochin, Chennai and Mahabalipuram. Now, leaving the city of Thanjavur, still quite awed by the ambience of its "Big Temple" (the world heritage listed Brihadishvara) we were ensconced in a friendly old Ambassador taxi, heading towards the city of Trichy (Tiruchirappalli). The lush Spring-green farming land, its animals with now-faded garlands, its smiling people, seemed lit with the colours and happiness of the recent harvest festival, Pongal, dedicated for Tamils to the sun-god, Surya.

It was only an hour's drive to Trichy where, circling the streets of the Rockfort area, we searched for the Hotel Royal Sathyam. Our increasingly distressed driver couldn't locate it, despite asking numerous rickshaw men, who are always familiar with the city. Finally, Julie spotted the large sign 'Sathyam' in the near distance: we enquired there. This was not the right hotel – it was a *sister* hotel to Royal Sathyam.

Subsequently, this memory became significant. For strangely, not only was Sathyam the hotel I later lived in for two weeks, but all these streets we circled in frustration were to become quite familiar to me. We did, at last, find the correct hotel, took the lift to reception, and were directed to our room on the hotel's 'first' floor. The lower floors being occupied by businesses and meeting rooms, and the car park basement set a half floor below ground level, the designated 'first' floor of the hotel was actually three stories above ground. This was to prove fateful.

Hotel Royal Sathyam

That evening, refreshed after the drive, we explored nearby Bazaar Road. It is a wonderful place, full of colour and life: bright emporiums displaying the glowing cotton fabrics of the region, myriad street stalls, people milling about in the coolness of evening, buying the essential of life – vegetables, shoes, cookware – or walking to the temple, crowding the road and narrow laneways. We found the restaurant I came to love and frequent, Vasanta Bhavan on NSB Road, overlooking the great water tank of Rock Fort Temple. Julie was enraptured by its rose-lassi drinks!

Saturday, January 25

As surely for anyone else in Trichy with religious or tourist purposes, entering the enormous Sri Ranganathaswamy temple was our first calling. By auto-rickshaw we went to Srirangam, the Kaveri River island site of this largest Hindu temple complex in India. Within the gateway, the outer circuits are full of commerce, bustling with people buying and selling, with pilgrims, beggars, family groups, tradesmen, musicians. Yet several days would be needed, and the help of a guide – which we usually resist – to fully appreciate these vast environs.

Column detail at the Sri Ranganathaswamy Temple

The complex extends beyond the huge gopurams arching the entrances, and into the *mandapams* (long pillared and carved stone hallways) towards many temples and shrines, culminating in the inner sanctum of one of the most revered forms of Vishnu, which gives the temple its name. As non-Hindus we could not enter this sacred chamber. But even as we passed within the outer layers, to our amazement and delight, the doors of the large shrine of Garuda serendipitously opened before us in the central pillared court. Perhaps this vision of the great human-headed bird, 'vehicle' of Vishnu, was a mark of events to come when considering an important dream Julie related to me some months before, in our early weeks in Malaysia. I will explain this portent, and the dream, further on.

The bustling ambiance and the grandness of Sri Ranganathaswamy was absorbing, yet that day we also wanted to visit another temple of significance on this island: Sri Jambukeswarar. Towards its main entrance the length of the street was smiled upon, with studied charm, by huge poster images of MGR (M. G. Ramachandran), Tamil Nadu's famous film-star politician.

Bemused by this, we passed under the front gopuram, a high cascading tower studded with thousands of multicoloured deities and their associated companions. Inside this liminal, amongst swaying palms, it felt quiet; eternally disconnected from the hubbub of pedestrian life without. The first, outer courtyard was a verdant enclosure of soft trees and flowering shrubs. Through consecutive walled courtyards, each with gopuram entrances and beautiful greenery, the path led on, deeper and deeper into the inner sanctum. The effect was to serially scale off the outer worldly concerns, ushering into a cool, massive-pillared temple: a dreamlike sensation.

Entrance to Sri Jambukeswarar Temple

Reaching this quiet internal space, but again as non-Hindus unable to access the inner sanctum, we followed another pillared hall, towards a small shrine dedicated to Saturn – which they call Shani. A Brahman priest welcomed us, offering the daub of *kumkumam* on our brows, and with a further spur of inspiration, presented us with flowers from the *murti*, the image of the deity. After a small unsure hesitation, we accepted this gift. What choice was there? Certainly, this India trip was not just a holiday.

Shani is one of the most diligently propitiated deities of Hinduism, especially in Tamil Nadu. He represents the acquisition of wisdom through arduous experience, having the same meaning in both Indian and Western astrology.

Pillared hall at Sri Jambukeswarar Temple

The passageway leading out from this shrine through walls, gopurams and courtyards, came to symbolise for me the stages of egress from the sanctum of our own forthcoming Saturnian event. The dry bare-footed steps we trod that day, in leaving the deceptively prosaic mood of this temple, were to become prophetic. It mirrored the same path I had travelled thirty-five years earlier, enduring India's trademark death-initiation when I nearly perished from amoebic dysentery, only returning to functional normality a decade later. Julie was now to submerge into those same opaque waters.

I was often to reflect upon this gift from the Saturn shrine in the coming weeks – was this a curse or a blessing? Perhaps what befell us was destiny, or karma if you like, and the *prasad* – the flower offering

– of Saturn was a blessing that allowed us, ultimately, to pass through the crucible with complete recovery, even if indelibly marked.

Priest at Saturn Shrine

Michael and Julie across from Saturn Shrine

Sunday, January 26

Today, we climbed the 437 steps on a massive outcrop that holds the Rock Fort Temple, up to the top shrine of Vinayaka, or Ganesha, who symbolises wisdom and the removing of obstacles: the god of new beginnings. It was a public holiday, a beautiful sunny day, the hilltop filled with families and groups of young friends relaxing on the stone steps and boulders, laughing, eyeing the scene, enjoying the cool breeze of the heights overlooking the city. After this day, I was never able to return to this unique site, despite living nearby for the next month – my legs were never again capable of the climb. Still, I often entered into the ground level shrine during this time, for a personal *puja* (ceremony).

Rock Fort Temple view

Descending from Rock Fort Temple, we crossed trafficked streets to find the beautiful Our Lady of Lourdes Church. In its quiet, cool interior, we sat recovering from the noise and heat outside, calmed by the ambience of gentle pink columns and archways, the glowing stained-glass windows. Its tall neo-Gothic spire is illuminated each year for the special Feast Day on the 13th of February, and although two weeks later I witnessed this display, due to my hand injuries I was unable to use a camera to record the sight. But the church made a wonderful vision at night, when looking out from the Vasanta Bhavan restaurant.

This Sunday, returning to the hotel room, we rested for the afternoon. Around 4pm, after ordering tea, we began checking our computers, and preparing for the evening. But suddenly, a new dramatic saga unfolded upon us with a thunderclap.

Our Lady of Lourdes Church

The Fire

A loud crack, then another, came from outside. Next door was a vacant lot, where men would escape the busy street to piss in the bushes or sleep though the midday heat. Beside the hotel stood a large, odd electrical contraption, which I later discovered to be a transformer, although unlike any transformer I've ever seen. One of the wires sparked loudly. This felt disturbing, but it was on the vacant lot, after all. It may have a connection to the hotel – but what, exactly, was not clear.

Our room at the Hotel Royal Sathyam

Puzzled by these events outside, I went to Reception to assure that nothing was amiss. There were no concerns there, although they were aware of the incident outside. Returning to our room, I watched from the window as a group of men stood around the structure, which continued to spark and crack. Finally, one man emerged from the bushes with a bent iron bar and used it to hit a lever, halting the sparking. Later, I heard that no-one had dared approach closely enough to switch it off, so the bar had been used to do that – an unbelievably dangerous action risking electrocution, but in this case he survived.

Again, I walked along the corridor to Reception, asking if all was well. It appeared to be 'business as usual'. Yet some Indian women were hurrying down the stairs; in hindsight, it was clear they knew something, and were getting out. But nothing was said to us, and there was no further indication of problems just then.

A few days later, I heard that when the outside transformer was shut down, hotel staff had attempted to restart the generator in the basement, when it sparked, due to excess electrical surge in the line. After turning it off, and attempting to switch back on, the power board ignited. There were in truth, very few flames, but a huge discharge of acrid smoke. The power board being at the base of the stairs, putrid black smoke drifted straight up into the hotel. With the lift out of action, these stairs were the only way out.

In our room, we were oblivious to this emergency in the basement. Suddenly, a man thrust open our door, looking wildly as smoke poured in, and told us to open the window. It was already open. We dressed quickly. Though Julie suggested we pack our bags before we left, there was no time: I urged her, "Just grab a torch and go."

The hotel corridor was pitch black. We found how dark it can be indoors when smoke-filled. Torches are all but useless. We reached the stairs quite nearby, but couldn't even see to descend into that cavernous inky pit – besides, we felt sure we'd find fire at the bottom. Rushing back to our room, also smoke-filled by now, we shut the door and ran to breathe at the open window, hanging there, looking down at the crowd on the vacant block, three floors below. They stared up at us with unease and curiosity, seeming unsure what to do, all alert to the drama.

Julie, in consternation, called to the upturned faces for help. Pressing her to stay calm while we found a solution, I admit to having been stunned by two things.

Firstly, how could this have happened so quickly? I am familiar with fire, and such a volume of smoke could only have issued from a considerable blaze, yet there hadn't been enough time for such a conflagration. Were the whole lower floors ablaze? It was completely impracticable that could have happened so fast. (I was not familiar with electrical fires.) I instinctively felt we had precious little time. Already, we had become trapped by delaying and mustn't wait longer.

Secondly, looking from the window, I saw no way of descending safely. How on earth were we to escape? We were in India, where the likelihood of a fire engine or extension ladder arriving in time was remote. On scanning the side of the building, it was clear there was no possibility of clambering down using structural features. I knew Julie could never scale down like a rock climber, anyway.

What a great relief it was then to see, suddenly, a thick rope descending from above. This was lowered to the ground then swung across to our window, directly within reach. But Julie, being no trapeze artist either, was unlikely to scale down three floors on a rope! Then I noticed that the rope-end had a bar attached so that, ideally, a person could sit on the bar while holding onto the rope. Someone above would then lower them to the ground. A fine idea, if there was a possibility it could happen.

I processed a fast succession of thoughts. The rope's bar-end lay on the ground. Would it be raised to our window? Apparently not, as I waited a little before debating an alternative action. Who was up above, anyway? South Indians are mostly of a slighter build than we large Australians – would one, or even two, be strong enough to lower us? With a raging fire below, how long would anyone stay on the roof? How much time did we have to see what transpired? If the rope disappeared for any reason, we were completely trapped. This was a critical moment: we had the rope now, not to use it felt suicidal, as it could quickly vanish.

Reaching out and pulling on the rope, I realised it was well secured above, which was promising. We looked at it dangling so close outside the window. We both knew this was never going to work, but our options had run out. It was a predicament with no obvious answer.

Believing the only choice was to grasp the opportunity offered, and find solutions as we went, I climbed from the window onto the rope, securing it twisted between my legs and feet, so my arms would not have to take the full weight. What to do next?

I said to Julie, "Climb out, and hold onto me." It felt the only possible action left, unlikely as it was to work. At first she sighed, "You go, I'll stay here." "Don't be ridiculous!" I responded. She tried to come out through the window, and at first was frozen, saying she couldn't do it. I kept telling her she could, but she was in utter disbelief at the whole situation. Reaching one leg around my waist while still sitting on the windowsill, she put her arm over my shoulder. We were ready to try it. I took a firm grip with my legs and hands in expectation. She moved off the windowsill – I never felt her weight.

She fell backwards.

Looking down from our window – transformer to the right, scaffolding (left) – added later, as part of the fire escape measures put in place

From a later observation by a friend in Australia, I realised she had fainted from extreme fright and stress. Looking down quickly, I saw her hit the wire which had sparked earlier, between our floor and the earth below. This jolt straightened her out, then she dropped the rest of the way, hitting the ground and lying in a classic 'dead person' posture. I knew she had been killed.

In disbelief that this could happen, all I could think was to get to her as fast as possible. I slid down the rope at breakneck speed, only to realise about two thirds of the way down that you can't do that with bare hands on hessian rope! The pain as my skin was ripped off by rope-burn became so severe that, believing I was within reasonable height from the ground, I dropped the rest of the way. That last fall sprained my right ankle and I fell back, hitting my head on rocks. I scrambled up quickly, across to Julie. Others were also rushing to her.

Hotel side. Our room was window second from left, first row.

Her head lay in a pool of blood on a small piece of concrete, with blood seeping from her mouth. Not thinking carefully, after clearing a large blood clot from inside her mouth, I grabbed her arms and with many keen assistants, we lifted and carried her across the ground towards the gateway. About half way I became concerned she might be choking on blood, so shouted, "Put her down!" That took some effort, as my helpers didn't understand English, nor why I would want to stop. I checked her mouth again, and for the first time, heard her groan – she was alive!

Assured there was no further mouth discharge, we carried Julie again but my grip felt strange and slippery. I looked at my hands – they were a bleeding, skinless mess from the rope burns.

Reaching the roadway, we slid her with difficulty into the side of an auto rickshaw. We should have waited for an ambulance to come, as the risk of spinal injuries was high, but in my shocked state, I wasn't awake to that thought. Once in the auto, I tried with my slippery hands to pull Julie onto the floor. Unable to grip adequately, but with her torso mostly in, I held her legs propped up and the rickshaw shuttled off down the road. To my surprise, we drove just around the next corner, as a hospital was nearby.

Amidst copious yelling, and many onlookers, a mechanical stretcher arrived. Julie was expertly lifted onto it, then wheeled away into the building, while dazed and blood-soaked, I followed up the ramps to the second floor and into the Intensive Care Unit (ICU).

GVN and Hotel Sathyam

GVN Hospital fronts onto a stony road, the bitumen cracked away into holes and rocky dirt, making mud-puddles in the rain. Walking past, one would never know a hospital was there. Outside, a nondescript pharmacy fronts the street. Secreted between that and a rather good chai shop is the upward sloping entrance, where I must stoop to avoid knocking my head when passing through. Julie was wheeled up this passageway.

Entrance to GVN Hospital

The whole hospital complex surrounds an inner courtyard containing a small Vinayaka shrine to which a priest arrives each Friday for puja, attended by many of the hospital staff. I came to know this shrine well over the next month. Vinayaka is the main deity of the Rock Fort Temple where we'd climbed the previous day. Julie was wheeled through this courtyard to the back of the building, up the ramp to the ICU on the third floor, where she was transferred to a bed. I followed along – bedraggled and covered in blood which soaked my white clothes.

The nurses asked me to move away while they attended their patient. She was wearing one of her favourite dresses, blood-stained and clinging to her body – they cut it off. Two days later I realised it could have been washed and repaired but it was too late. It had been thrown out.

I stood at the other end of ICU with nothing to do but wait, for hours holding up my grisly hands so they wouldn't ache, or drip everywhere. The doctor finally came to explain that Julie was all right except for sustaining wrist, jaw and rib fractures. This was a tremendous sense of reprieve. I had nowhere to go, so eventually was offered an ICU bed to lie down. I became increasingly cold.

Street outside GVN Hospital

Staff from the hotel arrived, wanting to assist me in some way. Distressed at the state of my clothes, they went out to buy a new shirt. As time passed though, I became so cold that I put my bloody white shirt back on over the new one, which upset them when they came to take me to a hotel. I didn't understand why they were concerned, not realising how particular Indians are about appearances, and especially blood with its associations of cultural impurity. This was to cause problems when we left the hospital.

At first, we went to the Hotel Susee Park, adjacent to GVN. Standing on the hotel front steps about 10pm as a small crowd gathered to stare at me, Sathish, the man from my hotel whom I later came to know well, argued with the manager of the Susee Park to provide a room. He flatly refused, saying they were full. Sathish pleaded with him that this was an emergency, but to no avail. Later, he explained that the manager refused me a room because of the attention my blood-soaked clothes generated from the bystanders. Affronted by what I saw as poor behaviour by the Hotel Susee Park, I resisted visiting their restaurant until weeks later (it turned out to have good food!)

Sathish took me to the Sathyam Hotel, the one Julie had spotted on our arrival at Trichy, where I remained for two weeks. We passed by the Royal Sathyam and retrieved a few items from our room. A day later, the rest of our luggage was brought here. It lay along the wall, untouched for about a week as my hands were too injured, smearing blood at every contact.

At night, I had difficulty in placing my hands comfortably anywhere in bed; they pained continuously. Paracetamol helped me to sleep. Serous discharge marked my clothes. Much that we normally take for granted requires the use of our hands, but when the palms and fingers are stripped of skin even the smallest action becomes an obstacle. A difficult task was tying up my pants. I was wearing tie-up pyjama whites but found it painful to knot the cord, and soon the top of my pants and the pockets were blood-stained. Worse still was cleaning myself after using the toilet. I couldn't risk infection by wetting my hands in the usual Indian method of using water, so what to do? Toilet paper stuck to my hands, so was mucky and useless. Finally, I solved the problem by using a bidet spray which, luckily, some Indian hotel bathrooms have installed, only appearing in use once Indians converted to pedestal toilets.

One day, I became sufficiently concerned for my hands that I decided to wash them in a bucket of salty water. I did this twice but the pain was unbearable, so scrapped the idea and took antibiotics instead. On showing my hands to the hospital doctors, they wiggled their heads in a "yes-no" sort of way and gave me iodine spray. They weren't concerned, and I felt capable of self-treating. We discussed bandaging my hands but finally agreed that open-air healing was best, so long as I controlled for infection.

To commute between Hotel Sathyam and GVN Hospital, I took an auto-rickshaw. Having to bargain hard each time became an annoying ritual. On many occasions though, the Royal Sathyam Hotel General Manager, Mani, organised his driver to transport me back and forth. The men from the Royal Sathyam Hotel were consistently supportive and, feeling personally affected by our circumstances, they could not do enough to help me. Often Sathish would phone, sometimes late at night, then send a car to collect me because 'madam' or the doctors were asking for me. These friends were truly a wonderful and essential assistance throughout the whole time Julie was in GVN. It's true they had a duty of care because of the fire, but their support and concern went far beyond that.

GVN Hospital, Singarathope, is one of three hospitals set up by Dr. G. Viswanathan to administer to the poorer classes. It is a private hospital but there was a remarkable appreciation among the people around Singarathope for the benefit GVN provides the community. Everyone had nothing but high praise for this facility.

Meanwhile, I was hobbling between hotel and hospital on a severely sprained ankle. Climbing and descending stairs was difficult but easier than trying to open lift doors with my hands. At GVN, a special lift was kept for patients and the elderly only, of which I availed myself thankfully for the first two weeks. The lift operator was a pleasant, friendly woman, always asking after me and Julie. She constantly checked my hands and was most concerned whether I was eating, which for the first three days I hadn't been able to do at all. My appetite had completely vanished – I felt nauseous even to think of food.

Later, it was clear I was suffering from shock during these early days. That explains much about my physiological anomalies: feeling chilly, lacking appetite, having a sense of disassociation. Finally, once I was ready to eat, I limped around to Vasanta Bhavan on NSB Road for late breakfast and dinner. The waiters there also were comfortingly concerned, regularly checking the healing of my hands.

GVN Intensive Care Unit (ICU)

Monday, January 27 (day 1)

Arriving at the hospital early in the morning, exhausted after only two hours sleep due to my injuries, I found Julie unconscious. She had been sedated to assuage the shock but it was not easy for me to see her lying, face misshapen by tubes inserted in her mouth and nose. The test results were coming in, showing that primarily she had sustained fractures, though the CT scan also revealed a small bleed in the left brain. The doctors think the bleed is not serious. Two of the fractures – the left mandible and right wrist – they want to operate on in a day or two, to fix plates for bone healing. I was anxious that a full anaesthetic operation was planned so soon following her trauma, wishing to see her awareness surface before 'going under' again.

Tuesday, January 28 (day 2)

Julie finally awoke and recognised me. I was so relieved! She couldn't talk, but once a few tubes were removed it was a big improvement seeing her face not so distorted. Tricia Martino, the Australian Consul from Chennai, phoned, having found out about the accident from newspapers in Australia. Somehow, they had tracked me down. The consulate people were supportive, offering to do anything they could to help.

People everywhere were spontaneously caring. I was told many were praying in the mosque, church and temples for Julie's recovery.

Wednesday, January 29 (day 3)

Julie recognised me again, and reaching out, took my hand and pressed it. This was a great consolation but I had to ensure that she grasp the wrist only, as my hands were still a mess. Every time entering ICU, I applied alcohol wash, but only on the backs of my hands and forearms. Alcohol on my palms was not exactly pleasant.

ICU permit me to enter at any time, which isn't allowed for other family members, who may only visit for an hour in the morning and evening. Most of the time I just walk in, change my street shoes for thongs and sit beside Julie. Though often sleeping, occasionally she wakes and looks at me. Later, she would see me as soon as I arrived and her eyes would light up with pleasure.

Questions arose in my mind as to whether Julie was in a suitable hospital. We knew of untreatable multi-resistant bacteria in Indian hospitals, and I felt, if this is not a quality hospital we should relocate. But I wasn't in a position to make comparisons, or evaluate GVN. The main critical-care doctor in ICU is Dr. Shiva, who is exceptionally competent. As Julie was not in a condition to be moved, I just trust this place is capable.

Contacting our travel insurance company, I found they are onto our case, even before validation of the cover activation, which has now been completed. They have established connections with the main orthopaedic surgeon, Dr. Senthil, who is also the head of the hospital. This is a good sign that action is progressing behind the scene.

The doctors want to perform the bone-fixing operation on Julie's wrist and jaw but it will require a full anaesthetic. I am not happy about this. It is only three days since her fall, and she hasn't adequately revived. Undergoing a general anaesthetic this soon felt too brutal to her consciousness. I sought out Dr. Senthil, who was stationed in Outpatients most of the day. He does this every day, attending to those who come in from the street with their health problems. The people waiting are seated in a large anteroom for a long time, biding their turn. I am favoured, allowed to stand at the front as next-in-line. This queue-jumping privilege makes me uncomfortable but thankful nonetheless. Each time I speak to Dr. Senthil like this, he always looks tired. He is happy to converse with me and even related the time he spent in Australia, at Lismore and Melbourne hospitals. He speaks excellent English and is refreshingly intelligent. Acknowledging my concerns, he explained there was no medical reason to delay the operation, but to accommodate my wishes they will defer the operation for another day. This was consoling for me, trusting on pure intuition.

Julie's condition continues as a serious concern. She has been taken out of critical care and is off the ventilator. Her vital signs are good – heart, lungs, blood pressure, temperature – but the fractured ribs and brain injury remain a primary focus. The small bleed in the brain was contained so should not present further problems, yet the rib fractures possibly can become a source of infection and develop blood pooling in the pleura. A central venous catheter (CVC) will be installed at her neck, instead of using the cannula method. The catheter may be an infection risk but in her situation it is necessary.

I was anxious that in the event of a serious downturn, what would be the fall-back plan? The insurance people replied that various possibilities were in consideration but that she was in no state for transfer, as the stress would be detrimental. I just pray it will progress well. Julie looks surprisingly strong, which was to reassure me in the months to come. From the beginning, her prospects for recovery looked good to me. Yet there were to be many hurdles and thresholds of despair ahead.

By this time, I had opened Julie's computer and discovered an email she hadn't sent, which was written as the sparks were exploding outside the window. In it, she had a premonition of the 'Indian situation' wherein things didn't always go to plan. We were well acquainted with that! I also accessed her Facebook page (not being on Facebook myself) and began telling her friends of the unfolding drama. This was the easiest way to keep people informed of developments. I updated the conversation three or four times a day. I had little else to do. Constantly moving back and forth between hotel and hospital each day became my repetitive, restricted circuit.

Aside from limping gingerly around to my favourite restaurant, there was nothing else to pass the day except washing, sleeping and conversing with friends online. I was extremely thankful for their sustained support. As more people heard about the accident, a few contacts were added – not *too* many, as she has always been selective about her 'friends' list. I maintained that diary of reporting until she eventually left hospital in Australia, four months later. It stands as a blow-by-blow telling of Julie's epic struggle, though little was conveyed then about my own journey, which shall be added here. Mostly, this book remains my direct account written at that time, when I was still suffering from shock and the exhaustion of constant concern for Julie's life.

Also, on a pre-existing internet forum of my own I began posting about Julie's situation. The members of this forum have a deeper understanding of my personal perception of the world and of our place in it, so were able to offer unique support. A separate folder was opened, where those with experience in remote healing were able to assist me. As well, people were sending healing energy from many places – here in Trichy, in Australia and from her friends across the world. It was amazing when people told me that their church or temple, and themselves personally, were praying for her. The abundance of spiritual energy we were receiving felt truly heartening. One man from the Royal Sathyam Hotel, in entreating Julie's recovery, shaved his head and undertook a small pilgrimage to the famous Samayapuram Mariamman Temple some distance from Trichy.

Since the accident, I have had instinctive visions of a great protecting wing that covers Julie. This vision, along with finding that her injuries were limited to healable fractures, and the enormous spiritual support she was receiving, made me realise that I was in the right position to claim an intent: that Julie would make a complete recovery. Telling her precisely this, I stated it not as a hope, or belief, but as an *intent*.

My hands are showing signs of improvement, but each night I attend to suppuration that forms at the edges of the individual wounds. Despite taking antibiotics, there is still a risk of infection as the edges are becoming inflamed and sore. The best way to treat this is to use a needle, breaking open the infected pockets and pouring in a little iodine. The iodine dries quickly avoiding the bedclothes being stained, but my hands and leg ache through the night and I can only get to sleep by taking paracetamol.

Thursday, January 30 (day 4)

Julie was more awake today and said, "Thirsty." I told her of the messages and support from friends and those in Trichy. In the morning I was visited by Ram, Goki's brother. Vartika and Goki are Julie's Facebook friends who we'd first met in Sydney some time ago. Goki's family lives in Trichy, so he had contacted Ram, who dropped by my hotel to see if there was any help he could offer. That was most appreciated.

During the day, Julie asked for me twice, which was relayed via Sathish, the ever-helpful manager from the hotel. All she wanted was water and to sit up. She was to undergo surgery in the evening, so we were unable to quench her thirst as it is not allowed to drink before general anaesthetic.

About 6pm Julie was wheeled off to surgery, which lasted three hours. Sitting in a little waiting room during this time, I was accompanied by a supportive group of my Indian companions. I assured them they could leave if they wished, that it was not necessary to accompany me while waiting for Julie to leave surgery. But it was unthinkable for them to leave a friend alone in a stressful situation. Ram was there, with his friend Ambu, and a young relative, Rajkumar. Sathish and Ethi, both managers from the hotel, also sat with me. Even the lift lady joined us for a while. We had a good conversation to pass the time; I felt they were trying to distract me from the tension of the situation.

During the evening, Ethi became anxious. He eventually revealed that his wife was expecting a baby and had been rushed off to hospital, leaving his young son at home. He was torn between staying with me and joining his wife. I urged him, "Don't be stupid Ethi. Go to your wife." He stayed anyway, for some time, before he left to see her. I gathered later that this had been a false alarm, and there was talk of a caesarean if she didn't deliver naturally. She delivered the baby a few days later, and all turned out well for them.

Mani (General Manager) and Ethi (Operations Manager) of Hotel Royal Sathyam

During our vigil my friends talked of other evacuation dramas that had happened at the hotel during the fire. Three hundred people escaped over the roof to another building – pity they hadn't informed us about that route! The receptionist was forgotten in the furore, so someone had to reach her and help her escape down the rope, but by that time they were using the attached sitting-bar correctly. Another foreigner I'd met had escaped from the window, clambering down structural features on the outer wall. I had looked for these myself at the time but there were none near our window.

Julie was wheeled from the operating theatre sometime after 9pm. It was distressing to see her pass by but I told myself that, no doubt, people always look terrible following an operation. Following her into the ICU ward, I asked how it had gone. "No dramas" was all the nurses said. I left for the hotel but my friends didn't want me to travel alone, feeling it was too dangerous at this time of night. Sathish, always by my side during these times at the hospital, organised a 'safe' rickshaw and young Rajkumar accompanied me on the ride. The hotel paid the fare, as they often did. Physically and emotionally exhausted, I collapsed into bed.

Friday, January 31 (day 5)

Morning

Julie looked considerably improved this morning. Her face had resumed its familiar appearance – it hadn't looked too good after the operation. She was conscious but not speaking yet, as she is on post-operative pain killers. Her red blood count was down to 6, and 10 is preferred, so she may need to be given blood. That was something I was hoping we'd avoid, this being India, where infections can easily accompany blood donations. But in the circumstances there is no alternative.

Afternoon

During the day she was annoying and demanding. One time she mumbled something like "water". "What did you say?" I asked. "WATER!" she yelled hoarsely. And later, "Help me get up. Where are my shoes? I have to get out of here." Before I departed at night she said to me, "I want a cup of tea."

Dr Shiva was in a bind. Due to the bleed in her brain, he was unable to introduce blood thinners but there is a risk she could develop Deep Vein Thrombosis (DVT). I am less worried about this because of her restless legs. They have wrapped her legs in a pressure bandage, which they kept doing for days. Some nurses are better at the wrapping technique than others, causing amusement for me to observe.

After taking ultra-sound tests on her intestines and checking her pelvis, the doctors were satisfied that all was well. It was only later they informed me that she had a fractured left pelvis, yet Julie never complained of pain.

Night

Around 8:30pm, Sathish rang. Julie was asking for me, and a rickshaw was sent to my hotel. The nurses must have contacted him. When

I arrived, she was agitated – glad to see me but kept asking, "Where am I?", "How did I get here?" and, "Get me out of here!"

I tried to explain she had had a fall, and was in a good place, and to trust that all was going well. But I wasn't sure she would remember, or that she may wake up later in the same state of frightened disorientation. I looked around for somewhere to sleep – in one of the ICU beds perhaps? I told Sathish he should go home but he doesn't listen, and stands around attending to any little problem that arises, like getting a nurse's attention.

Then, in came three new patients who were in serious conditions – the last one was screaming and fighting. Dr. Shiva took it all in a night's work, directing the nurses and joking with colleagues, who began arriving to attend the new emergencies. The place was in turmoil but not chaotic, and I realised they could need the spare beds at any time. Besides, it would be an impossibility sleeping in here with the noise and lights.

Julie went through the usual process of wanting water – the nurse tilted the bed up higher so she could drink from a bottle. This put pressure on her chest, causing pain from the fractured ribs. She wanted to know why she had pain in her side. I explained again about the fall and broken ribs. Next, she wanted to know where she had fallen from – for the first time, we were engaging in a conversation!

With help from Sathish we were able to attract attention from the busy nurses to obtain water, and to lower the bed. She kept asking to have it lowered but so much was happening to the other patients, it took time. I am unable to do it myself, as it is a ratchet handle operation which my hands are too damaged to use. Once the bed was lowered she immediately became calmer.

Then she asked me, "Where are you staying?" This was the first time she had asked a question about me, indicating she was returning to her usual self. Also, I could see her caring sentience re-emerge in the way she was responding, transitioning from her own immediate, essential needs. She appeared to be retaining memory of what she was told. Not wanting to say too much in response to her enquires about what happened, in case it brought back traumatic memories, I told her I would explain more later. Then she said to me, "You can go now." I took this as a genuine awareness of the situation, whereas previously she exclaimed that I must not leave her in this weird place. Finally, she settled, and on clarifying some requirements to the nurses, Sathish and I left. No further calls came for me through the night.

During the evening, the neurosurgeon had come in to see the other patients. He examined Julie, and after explaining to him that she had been frightened, with no memory of how she got here, he nodded and said, "Yes, Post Traumatic Amnesia. It is to be expected." Little did I know then, that casual off-hand remark was naming one of her biggest obstacles to recovery.

Saturday, February 1 (day 6)

They took Julie off ventilation again but left the tubes in, and connected her to a reduced level of oxygen support techniques. Dr. Shiva explained that the reason for her agitation and heart fibrillation, which had occurred earlier, was a collection of thick sputum in her throat. He said head-impact patients can have difficulty clearing their throat, so the intubation machine addresses that condition. It also controls oxygen levels but they have to clear her passages periodically with a suction tube inserted down various channels – a horrible, distressing procedure. Later, she had another small agitation but tube repositioning and further suction calmed her.

The duty doctor told me he thinks she is depressed. I replied "I'm not surprised." Julie has always disliked illness, and as an emotional person she goes through the whole range of moods associated with an ailment.

She was looking more unsettled this evening than earlier in the day. I was able to reach Joan Anderson, her cousin, on the phone from Australia, using the loudspeaker. Joan had a short one-way talk to her – Julie can't speak normally yet. She was aware and reassured to hear Joan's voice.

The doctors are impressed with her body strength. They say she broke the fall first with her right hand, then her left hip (that must have been something in itself), then her left chest, and lastly her head. They tell me any Indian would have crushed their bones, especially someone over forty, falling from that height (Julie was 61).

Sunday, February 2 (day 7)

Afternoon

Julie is not progressing as well as the doctors have expected. Though not declining, holding steady, by now they would prefer to see better progress. They don't appear to know why this is happening. We can accept that from the concussion and operation, she will naturally take time to recover. She was sustained on the oxygen machine (intubation) for 48 hours but when that was removed there were difficulties. By the time I arrived back at the hospital she had been sedated while repositioning her mouth tubes. The tubes had been irritating her mouth and she was trying to push them out. This afternoon she is off the intubation machine, and breathing with only a small oxygen nose tube.

At this point, it would be enlivening for Julie's spirit to be awoken more, so I'll try anything to remind her of what she loves. The doctor suggested music from her earphone player could help. That is a problem, because not only will I need to choose appropriate music to put on it, but I'm sure she would not be capable of keeping the earphones in place. Headphones will need to be sourced from somewhere, and her Hindi lessons cleared from the player. Not just being in no state to learn a new language, but they don't speak Hindi in Tamil Nadu, so she won't be wanting to listen to them.

Night

Dr. Shiva was looking perplexed tonight. He didn't have an answer. He told me she is not improving, though not deteriorating ... just stable. The pooling of blood from her rib fractures was one reason for his concern, as her energy and oxygen were being consumed by this condition. Yet that didn't explain everything. He is at an impasse, and I know why. He can only heal the body, which he is doing, but Julie's spirit is at a gateway where no one can help. This is between her spirit and the infinite. She must find the answer she needs – that is why she came to India. This is the night we have been waiting for since we decided to come on this journey. This is where she wanted to reach, and tonight she is there. I told her, "I love you Julie."

Late Night

I have asked my online friends to cease remote healing efforts altogether. Julie has reached a critical threshold. It is not just the blood pooling. She is going through a passageway from which only she can exit. Interference from me or my friends is now counterproductive. This is a difficult moment for me, as I am a 'solutions' person who never gives up looking for answers. To stand back and watch as my loved one battles alone is distressing. I have to let her go – if she doesn't want to live then I cannot bind her to me, or life, with my love. This has to be her choice, between her and that which awaits on the other side of death's door. If she wants to leave, it is her right, and this is the time for that choice. Everything she requires is standing waiting for her decision. We will know what that is in the morning.

GVN ICU Week 2

Monday, February 3 (day 8)

Morning

Walking into ICU this morning, it was obvious to me that Julie was looking better. This was so gratifying. The decision had been made in her subconscious overnight: she was back in the land of the living, ready to go through whatever was required. During the first week in ICU I assured her she would make a complete recovery, but she would have to step up to that – it wouldn't come without a fight. Seeing her this morning it was clear to me that she would make it, no matter what obstacles lay before her. The bid for life and recovery had been made, and that promise must be fulfilled, no matter what.

Her feet and calves are bandaged up to the knee for DVT prevention. These bandages keep unravelling because her legs are so restless. My hands are incapable of massaging but the tips of my fingers had escaped the skin stripping so, with them, I twiddle her toes.

Julie continues to slide down the bed and we have this procedure to yank her back up, during which I am useless to help. The 'lifting procedure' is, firstly, to call for Security, that being one of the men around the hospital who do the manual tasks as well as sitting in front of doors to keep families out. The nurses are slight, without the strength to pull Julie up themselves. Secondly, a ratchet is employed to lower the bed-head (when she is back in position, it is used to wind the bed-head back up). Next, the assistance of an older doctor in ICU is enlisted. He runs his own show at one end of the room, and is strong and stocky. With these two men, and a few nurses helping, from behind the bed-head they pull Julie back till she is at the top. This procedure happens many times a day as she constantly squirms her way down the bed into an uncomfortable position.

Afternoon

More was revealed today about the pelvis fracture which everyone, except Dr. Senthil the orthopaedic surgeon, thought was not critical.

This fracture is the most serious for Julie's immediate recovery, because she is not allowed to weight-bear on her leg for six weeks, meaning she cannot stand up from bed or walk to the toilet for all that time.

X-rays showed the blood pooling on her left rib cage had considerably increased, so a tube was inserted to drain two litres of fluid. That rallied her general well-being, and oxygen levels immediately jumped to 100 (full). But the ventilator was needed again, re-introducing tubes through her nose and throat, about which she is not happy. The rib cage drainage tube increases the risk of infection, requiring more antibiotics.

Evening

Julie revived during the day, and was at her meddlesome best. She was pulling the tubes out from her mouth and picking at the central venous catheter (CVC). She had been such a monkey they had to tie her hands down. I met Dr. Shiva while arriving in the evening, as he was about to depart on his black motorbike with black full helmet (Indians rarely use a full helmet, if any).

He stopped and took off his *lingam* helmet to explain what they had done that afternoon. The CVC was switched to another position, as leaving it too long in one place risked infection. She was off the ventilation machine and on the T-piece, meaning she was breathing on her own, with only added oxygen. This doesn't bother her as much as the other tubes. He said he will remove the T-piece tomorrow, which will allow her to speak, as well as take in food (cup of tea!)

My hands are covered in thick scabs, looking like battered fish, but ankles are beginning to heal. Tomorrow I move back into the old hotel, which is opening for business again. During the day I called in and they showed me our previous room. I asked about smoke alarms. They said these were being installed in the corridors. "The rooms?" I asked ... they smiled, which I took for a 'no'. I didn't ask if these were installed now, or were only aspirational. It is India after all.

Travelling in India one becomes accustomed to a high degree of self-responsibility and on-the-spot improvisations, as relying solely on systems for safety or comfort is inadvisable. I asked about fire escapes, and was told approval had been given to build exterior exits.

"Fine, but what about right now?" I asked. The stairs are still the only escape. They showed me the staff stairs at the end of the corridor, which lead down to the basement, and up to the roof. I wish I had known about them during the fire! Not feeling highly elated at this point, I asked about window escape. They assured me there is now a roll-down ladder, lowered from the roof. "Machine driven?" I asked, "No, manual, by hand" they replied. Well, I suppose that is something but two things concerned me: could they secure it over each window along the row, and how would Julie have climbed down a floppy ladder?

The external transformer has not been repaired, so the hotel will run on three reconditioned generators. I suppose it should be adequate, at least no worse than most hotels we stay at. Nonetheless, I doubt Julie will want to convalesce here, which I told them. They understood, and if it comes to that, we will probably try to get into the Hotel Susee Park which refused me the night of the drama. God knows what their fire procedures are.

It is definitely more convenient to stay at the Royal Sathyam than the Sathyam, being only a short walk to the hospital. Extensive work has been done to make the hotel safer in case of fire, or I would not even consider moving back. Although a typically Indian 'yes fine (probably)' approach, I was not taking risks – I had been watching and discussing with the General Manager all the alterations that were being undertaken for increased safety. This is not a budget accommodation but a good middle-range hotel.

Night

Julie is experiencing bladder discomfort, causing her to squince her face with pain. The doctors aren't sure what is triggering this but it could be the catheter tube-end irritating her internally. There is nothing they can do as it doesn't appear serious, and more analgesics are being avoided. The distress increased during the day. Incapable of speaking with all the tubes, she mouthed to me in no uncertain terms, "Get me out of here!" She didn't want me to leave tonight – she wanted me to get her out of the place, which I couldn't do. I had to leave her in pain, at the end.

Tuesday, February 4 (day 9)

Morning

The first attempt at helping Julie up from bed was undertaken this morning, and managed to have her sitting on the edge of the bed. It was so exhausting that she couldn't last long, but exhilarating nonetheless, to see her seated upright after a week of lying flat.

Afternoon

During the day she had to endure the lung clearing suction procedures, which are necessary with intubation. It is distressing but without it the breathing tube clogs up, which is even more distressing. When suction isn't sufficient, air with a little fluid is pumped down, bringing any lung congestion up into the mouth and making a horrible noise, which is equally unpleasant. Suction, in one form or another, is required about every hour. It is a barbaric business but there are few options when breathing through these tubes. I dislike watching but the nurses take it in their stride.

Evening

Around 5pm, Dr. Shiva came in and rallied everyone to take out the tubes: 'extubation'. This they did, after the preliminaries, while he, in his casual manner, sat down for his dinner. Once half-an-hour of gurgling and coughing by Julie had passed, she was patently more comfortable. Previously, her arm ties had been removed, but because she still tugs at the tubes, despite my explanations and admonitions, to restrain her arms a nurse has been stationed beside her all day. The nurses by this time had begun vying for Julie's 'liking' status.

With the mouth tubes detached, she's sitting more upright without chest pain: a major improvement. And she could speak, albeit quietly. By the time I left she was feeling better, with the promise of food and a cup of tea tomorrow. She had been calling me close and asking for things, like her dress, and commenting that she wouldn't be able to travel by car. She also wanted tonic water, a drink she often likes in India but which is not always available – unsure if it can be obtained in Trichy.

Before I left, she called me over, and whispered forcefully in her best Godfather husky voice, "Where's my tonic water!?"

Wednesday, February 5 (day 10)

Every day is so intense, so much happens, and Julie's condition changes constantly through the day. Also, many things are happening for me outside the hospital. It becomes tiring and stressful to keep on top of it all, along with my own ailments. The following is a good example of such a day, when weeks feel compressed into twenty-four hours.

Morning

This morning she has not exactly bounced back. Unable to sleep during the night, sedatives were administered around 3am, causing her to be drowsy during doctor's rounds at 9:30am. I heard from Mythili, one of the nurses, that she and Julie had talked for an hour after doctor's rounds, along with a cup of coffee, which she greatly enjoyed.

The mouth and nose tubes have been removed except for a less intrusive oxygen tube across her nose. I bought headphones from a tiny shop upstairs in a building which Sathish had shown me, and finally worked out how to assemble music on our little player which she hasn't used until now. I left her drowsily listening to music an hour ago.

I relocated back to the Hotel Royal Sathyam. It is definitely taking the fire issue seriously – restructuring in the basement, hammering and drilling, creating clouds of cement dust that I held my breath to walk through. Asbestos cement is commonly used in India. Engineers had been engaged to advise on what can be done by way of additional stairs, fire escapes and prevention. This hotel will be safer than all the neighbouring ones, thanks to our misfortune. Advantageously for me, it is so close to the hospital that I merely amble around the corner to visit Julie.

She isn't up to using a laptop yet and is still having waves of pain from the rib fractures, which aren't serious but face-grimacing nonetheless. This is to be expected and there is little that can be done. Th pain should subside gradually over the next week. She is not in a mood to receive phone calls, either. I will consider that later – hopefully her vocal capacity will improve in a day or two. The previous phase of friends just talking *to* her is not required now. She is awake and aware, looking around at the happenings in ICU. What she needs is to become more active.

Late Morning

Julie is the best that I've seen yet. During a short conversation she asked, "Is it true I fell?" Stepping through the short version again, she appeared to be taking it in. Just before I left she said, "I'm wrecked" – possibly as much from our conversation as everything else.

Late Afternoon

Her voice is husky but growing stronger. Along with increased alertness comes awareness of the noise in ICU. Indians generally are of a more vociferous culture than Australians. They speak at a loud volume most of the time, and when ICU is full, as today, with many relatives visiting and the nurses excited with the action, it can be overwhelming for Julie.

I put the head-phones around her ears without the music. But she took them off and said to me, "OK, let's go to the toilet." She's not pleased with the idea of pooing in bed, but I assure her that's how they do it in hospitals when you can't stand or walk. She isn't comfortable with that approach, on principle!

A new problem arises. With the intravenous sustenance-tubes removed, Julie has to eat, but what? She is not a fan of Indian food unless it is well prepared. She loved the food at Vasanta Bhavan the night we had dinner there before the fire, but basic restaurant or hospital fare leaves her feeling it's all 'hot brown mush'. When one is sick, familiar food is critical, yet where could that be sourced in Trichy? Tomorrow, I have the task of finding something enticing to eat. Perhaps the hotel could make up tomato and cucumber sandwiches but that will be on white bread. Mostly, Indians don't eat western-style bread, and when it is available it's always white. She can't live on that.

Vasanta Bhavan, my favourite restaurant, makes excellent varieties of fried rice, which I can bring back to the hospital. When Julie was sick in Varanasi I found ham and salad brown-bread rolls, but I've not found anything similar in Trichy as it is a 'holy' city, meaning fully vegetarian, and rarely frequented by Western tourists. This is going to go on for a while so some research is called for. Thankfully, the hotel and hospital canteen both make omelettes which are good for breakfast. One hurdle after another.

Parcel posting

During the day, along with everything else, I decided it was time to send a parcel home to avoid carrying excess weight on the planes. We had always intended to send a parcel back before we left but had expected to complete that in the peaceful sanity of Fort Cochin. After sorting through our luggage, I put a largish parcel together.

Posting parcels in India has recently become more complicated, as a directive went out to Post Offices that they must inspect the contents of parcels before dispatching. This has turned comical but also a great nuisance. In India, traditionally, parcel contents are well bound with twine, usually in plastic bags if possible to protect against water damage, and sometimes placed in a cardboard box. Then they are taken to a tailor to sew up with calico wrapping. This last part needs to be well done, or the parcel becomes loose and sloppy during the journey creating a danger of falling apart. On top of that, the stitching has to be sealed with wax!

But since the latest directive, contents are required to be first checked by the Post Office staff. This means bringing the contents in a box to the Post Office, requesting them to check it, then carrying to a tailor to sew up with calico. How it hasn't been realised you could put more in *after* the checking, making a complete farce of the security measure, is something one would only encounter in India.

Unfortunately, I was not in the best condition to manage the whole pantomime, so the hotel management were adamant they would help. Sathish undertook the task of going with me to the Post Office and ensuring it went well. They had sent many parcels (or so they said) and knew all about it. As we proceeded, it dawned on me that they didn't know as much about this as I did. But not having the stamina to take over the project, I allowed Sathish to run the show.

After considerable discussion in Tamil with everyone at the hotel, he decided to take me to the local Post Office, where he 'had a friend' – always a risky option, in my opinion. I suggested that the Main Post Office would be more likely to have tailoring services on hand. Unfortunately, Sathish only agreed with this once the drama at the local office was complete.

The local Post Office is situated at a corner on a busy main road, with a market on the opposite side full of restaurants and shops, selling everything imaginable. It was not a place I wanted to walk to in my current state. Julie and I had made an excursion along this crowded and disjointed footpath before the fire, and even then found it exhausting. Thankfully, this time Sathish and I availed ourselves of the Managing Director's personal car and driver, which, with some difficulty, dropped us off at the Post Office. Sathish went to the market to find a tailor, or at least materials for wrapping.

On returning, he revealed there were no tailors and he had purchased a stash of calico, stitching needle and twine, as well as sealing wax. But the calico was blue! "I couldn't find white", he said. And the twine was thick hessian, which would be impossible to use as stitching. This was becoming one of those Indian 'I-can't-believe-this-is-happening' experiences. Luckily, I had brought my own twine, along with a knife and felt pens for writing on the address, which I always carry with me in India. But would the black felt pen show up against the blue calico?

Sathish said his friend wasn't there but we could go in and start. His friend might turn up. I was in a state of disbelief at the way this was turning out – did he mean to stitch up the parcel himself? That is not an easy task for someone unskilled. Tailors make a bag of the calico first, on their machine, after measuring, and only hand stitch the last flaps. Also, it was getting late in the day, and the Post Office was closing soon.

The office staff were satisfied with the contents, and although at first concerned about the blue calico, following much head-wiggling discussion they decided it would suffice. Sathish began to stitch up the material. That's when I suffered a wave of despair and disbelief that I had allowed myself to be trapped in this insanity.

Amongst dispassionate staff conducting their languid Post Office business, we were behind the counter, scrambling on the floor with this swath of flapping material, and Sathish doing his best to gain a semblance of command over the task. It wasn't working. What could I do? I had to sit on a small stool they kindly provided, as my legs, knees and ankle were too sore to squat around the dishevelled beast of a recalcitrant parcel. And my hands were next to useless, still being a mass of unhealed scabs. But I had to do something, as Sathish was clearly making a complete hash of the job. I looked up in vain at the disinterested faces around us. Was there some way I could just crawl out of this situation?

I did help – I had to – with what little I could do, which wasn't at all good for my injuries. But to my surprise, Sathish was wrestling a degree of diminishing chaos out of the cloth blob – it almost looked as if he was going to come close to winning! The stitches were all over the place. But time was running out, and we had to stitch wherever a flap remained, and forget what it looked like. Once he had come close to finishing, I tidied it up at the end to obtain some tightness to the still sloppy blob of a parcel. With twine and calico strewn across the floor inside the office, we succeeded in getting the felt pens to display the addresses legibly enough, though Sathish had to dash out and buy another pen in the midst of it all.

Sathish's friend, who finally turned up, took the parcel into a back room where together they endeavoured to seal it with a candle and wax. Finally, the task completed to a base level of compliance, the calmly impassive yet friendly woman at the counter, who had sat there detachedly observing our frantic antics as if watching someone else's children in a sandpit, processed the paperwork and payments. We left the Post Office exhausted but relieved. That's when Sathish said to me, "It would have been better to take it to the Main Post Office!" I must say, ultimately Sathish did a superb job of accomplishing what had become a ridiculously impossible mission, even if we did go at it the hardest way. I only hope our dishevelled consignment reaches Australia without disintegrating. (It did!)

Evening

Two steps forward and one back. Away for an hour, and on returning, Julie has a fever. This means infection. They are bringing her temperature and heart rate down. Dr. Shiva is not sure what is the problem. "Is it in the urine, blood, lung? Is it malaria?" As he said that, my eyes rolled. When earlier they had to bring in blood, I worried we were stepping through into another layer of risk. Reassuringly, he informed me he now has excluded the possibility of malaria. Apparently, infection can sometimes enter from a blood transfusion. He has changed the antibiotics.

It goes to show that she is not yet free of the woods. The sooner the drain in the side of her chest is closed the happier I will be, but that may not be for two days or more, depending on the quantity of fluid that continues to drain.

She has been given a sedative, so she ought to sleep. As long as her breathing continues to supply enough oxygen, and the ribs heal, infection should be contained. After a week like this though, some contagion is only to be expected, which is a worry. It does indicate to me the need to be out of ICU as soon as possible, with all surplus-to-requirements holes sealed.

Night

I returned at 10:30pm. Julie was fine, apart from claiming the toilet system for bed patients "was crazy". Her fever had completely gone. Dr. Shiva shrugged, and said, "You see many things in ICU". Yet the danger of infection is still taken seriously, and tomorrow I hope for more indication of what happened; but for now, her voice has improved, and she's even practising on the breathing exercise toy, once we had worked out how to use it.

Now I'm the one who's wrecked. Up and down, left and right. One good thing though, is that amidst these infection concerns, Julie is improving in her physical capacity almost by the hour. She asked again, "When will we get out of here?" I explained that in a day or two she will be moved to a private room for a few quiet days. Does such a thing exist in this hospital? I'll contact the insurance people and push them to make sure it does. It all depends on how well she manages those breathing exercises. But personally, between you and me, I know Julie has powerful lungs.

As for food, I can relax – she will be kept on liquid foods again for another day. This sounds sensible. Hopefully, I can sleep now...

Thursday, February 6 (day 11)

Morning

The source of the infection has been found: the upper right lung. At least it's not malaria. It may have been initiated by the remnants of the smoke inhalation. A new antibiotic is prescribed which should control this pathogen but Julie has to cough up the phlegm, which is not easy in her constantly supine position. The doctors have provided a small blowing and sucking toy to exercise her lungs. They have impressed upon us how important it is to use this but she shows little interest. I have to keep passing it to her, and she tries a bit then gives up.

This morning the nurses helped her to sit on the edge of the bed again, which she found a little easier this time. Then the physio began slapping and thumping her upper-right back, which she did not enjoy. He also conducted the usual leg and wrist movements. Dr Senthil, ever vigilant, is keen to maintain flexibility in her right wrist, and each morning the cast is removed for physio treatment. Finally, the doctors decided she can have the cast permanently removed. I didn't think this was wise, as she often bangs her wrist against the bedside railing, to force me to release it so she can walk to the toilet. She hits the railing saying, "What's this thing? I can't get out of bed. Come on, drop it. I have to go to the toilet." And when I refuse she says, uncomprehending the situation and in frustration, "Oh, you're useless!" She still can't get used to the diaper method. She is not yet her normal self, so her reactions are a mix of being sometimes aware and conscious in her usual self, and other times instinctive and semi-conscious.

Solid food begins. Dr. Senthil advised that she should be eating proper food. He called the canteen chef to ICU, to speak with me and the always-present Sathish. Julie asked for *palak paneer*. They had no spinach (*palak*), so the chef was told to buy some. She needs protein, which the cheese (*paneer*) should provide, and the spinach will have iron. So with that, a sandwich, and a little pawpaw, she should begin to feel more normal. Sathish thinks the hospital canteen food will be cleaner than that of the hotel, where construction is ongoing.

This will be a big transition for Julie, to eat her own food. As for phone calls, she's not interested because of the effort to speak. She has said a little, though. For instance, when two nurses were doing things to her this morning while Vivek, the registrar, was standing with me on the other side, she softly observed to me, "These girls are hopeless." Vivek wanted to know what she said – I laughed and told him I'd explain later. She does like Mythili.

After all the morning activities Julie becomes exhausted. She is torpid until late afternoon and evening, when she sparks up and we can interact over food, photos, email readouts and chat.

Afternoon

What a change a bit of normality brings! This afternoon Julie ate a whole sandwich and some pawpaw. On returning, at about 5pm, I showed a few photos on the laptop, her Facebook page and emails. She didn't take much in but it brought back sufficient familiarity that she began talking to people. She had a conversation with Dr. Vivek, telling him that she found the ICU interesting, and she'd like to return and help them in some way. Then she talked with the nurses, especially Mythili, and wanted her to come to Australia (to visit her 'mother' in Australia, I heard her say). Mythili is the main earner in her family of mother and three sisters, and she won't be marrying until she sets her mother up with a house to live in. Julie told of her own mother's death two years ago, and how she still longs for her.

Next, she had a cup of chai and a little vegetable fried rice. She was gaily chatting away in her 'Godfather' voice, watching the people coming in at visiting hour. I was blown away – how quickly she had changed.

I don't expect this to remain consistent but hopefully, she is progressing. It is certainly reassuring. She has forgotten about Trichy, so tomorrow I will show the photos we took of this area before the fire, but first they must be transferred to her computer.

Night

Another step back. I was called to the hospital at 11:30pm. On arrival, I found Julie was in the CT scan room. Dr. Shiva appeared and explained she had had a mild heart attack. Julie noticed nothing of this – she was calm and clear, retaining her previous alertness. Dr. Shiva only picked it up from the ECG reading. All other signs were fine: blood pressure, heart rate, oxygen saturation, breathing rate. He did say it was not an actual heart attack but a myocardial ischemia feature in her ECG read. This has created a dilemma for the doctors who want to medicate, thinning the blood a little to avoid a clot, but thinning could cause complications if her brain bleed is still active. Hence, the CT scan.

The neurologist arrived and examined the scan report. He told me the brain bleed had settled down, so it could handle a small amount of anticoagulant. There's no concern about increased bleeding from the ribs as that is being drained, and anyway it can be monitored. So it felt safe to proceed with slight blood thinning, while watching for signs of increased bleeding, in which case they will stop. This will last for twelve hours, which must be a kind of risk period. Before I left, Dr. Shiva said that he would first consult with the cardiologist.

Meanwhile, I conversed with Julie who thought there was a lot of unnecessary fuss, while she was calm and collected. I didn't explain anything to her of the doctors' discussion. Dr. Shiva thinks the cause is bodily stress.

Now we are watching, to see if the heart will do another hiccup, or signs of bleeding. Her heart is showing, as it always has, strong and regular action, so it is hoped the myocardial ischemia feature is only a passing blip. And that the medications don't cause bleeding complications.

Friday, February 7 (day 12)

Morning

Julie had an omelette and tea, then finished a whole cheese and salad sandwich, more pawpaw and a cup of tea. Her revived appetite is a relief, as now she has to ingest her own nourishment, having consumed so little in the last two days. Knowing she has to eat, she is making an effort.

There is barely a sign of the previous evening's drama, though she was dopey during the morning. Dr. Senthil suggests she is not sleeping enough at night. I explained to him about Julie's sleep patterns, hoping they might try to help with this. Surely she requires relaxant medication, ICU being a busy, noisy and constantly lit place. It's no wonder she is having trouble sleeping. The monitors above each bed make a series of beeping sounds, which constantly go in and out of synch with each other, creating a spooky, electronic, disturbing, trance music – a perfect real-life Brian Eno composition!

The doctors are exemplary at keeping me informed of developments and considerations on Julie's condition, which I appreciate. The physician in charge of ICU, Dr. Baskaran, is always willing to discuss my concerns in his little office off to the side, and is also ready to act on them when we agree.

Julie keeps asking me if she we can take a hotel room for a few days – just the two of us – so she can recuperate. The seriousness of the situation remains beyond her comprehension.

Night

One of the things I find touching, here, is seeing the families of ICU patients who sit waiting all day on the corridor seats, and on the floor outside the doors. They are allowed an hour twice a day to visit, during which time they rush in and stand around the beds: solemn, crying, talking, silent. Attempting to enter at any lapse of security, when I walk through someone often tries to follow. Sometimes they are successful for a moment but mostly not. I feel guilty at my privilege of visiting at any time but nonetheless, am extremely grateful for it.

I've been to check on Julie at 10pm, and the families are still there, sleeping on the chairs and floor. They stay 24 hours. It is hard to imagine Australian families sleeping in the hospital corridors when one of their loved ones is in critical care. I know it is allowed in exceptional circumstances if a guest room is available, although I'm not sure how many Australian hospitals do that anymore. To see the determination of these people not to leave a family member in crisis, and their willingness to endure long hours of boredom and uncomfortable conditions, is one of the beautiful things I love about India.

Saturday, February 8 (day 13)

Morning

The physiotherapist came in around 10am and woke Julie, who had been sleeping in. This physiotherapy is her worst experience of the day. She is sat up on the edge of the bed, which she is finding easier now, while he pounds her right upper back to loosen the lung phlegm. This is excruciatingly painful for her, though of great necessity. Following more of the arm, fingers and legs movements, she lies back to recuperate. Hopefully, by 1pm she should be ready for tea and omelette. It is slow but steady progress.

The conversation has now turned to the chance of moving to a quieter room. Some of this delay relates to the rib drainage. Its daily volume is reducing, so possibly the tube may be removed tomorrow, at the earliest. There is discussion too of removing her bladder catheter.

In all, progress is positive, though not fast enough for Julie, who would like to be out of here as she finds ICU overwhelming.

Gina's flowers arrived! Gina is one of the admin staff at the School of Humanities, at the university in Armidale, our home in Australia, where Julie works as a research academic. Gina had been in touch with me about the correct address to send flowers, and although I was not optimistic, there they were when I walked in! It is amazing, as Fran, another of Julie's friends, had been unsuccessful in having roses delivered. It's hard to know what will work. Julie was pleased but I also told her of Fran's missing roses – she understood.

She is not at all pleased though with the toileting business. She demands help to get to the toilet, and scolds me when I tell her it's not possible. I understand. She does not enjoy the bed-diaper system and who can blame her – neither would I. This issue will be on top of my list for an alternative method. After all, as she's more stable now, she could possibly stand on her right leg and progress to a commode system. It would make a big difference to her mood and sense of self-control.

Evening

One of those unfortunate cultural misunderstandings occurred this evening. About 5pm when I arrived, Julie was looking better but still tired. I discussed her reactionary moods with Dr. Baskaran, who understood that she was depressed with the noisy, fussy scene in ICU. We talked about changing to a single room tomorrow. He suggested she could move for half an hour to a quieter room – at least that's what I thought he was saying. Seemed a good idea, so the plan was to do it post-visiting time.

Meanwhile, Mythili and I had organised the canteen to bring up a cup of vegetable soup, which Julie enjoyed, after which she ate a little fruit. But then she become tired from all the attention. She likes Mythili, who has a quiet, efficient, gentle and intelligent manner – Julie told her she was an angel. She would have gone mad if it weren't for Mythili taking over her day-time care. With everyone else, there is a cultural difference: they are more comfortable with joking, loud, brusque behaviour, whereas Julie prefers a peaceful atmosphere.

At last Dr. Baskaran said, "Will we do it? For just a half-hour?" Yes, Julie and I thought, why not – a change for only a short time would break the pattern.

Alas, we had misunderstood. Her bed was moved out into the little passageway, where it stayed, while she was sat up on the edge of the bed, a position that puts pressure on her ribs, to look out the window. Admittedly, it was a pleasant scene outside, if only she had had the strength to hold her head up and see it. The window overlooks the central courtyard of the hospital where the little shrine of Vinayaka sits, and a leafy neem tree grows up to the roof. Everyone crowded around the bed, helping her to sit, to hold her head up and look out, when she just longed to escape the noise and fuss.

I was dumbstruck, as Julie would have been, had she any energy. It was a difficult situation. After a sufficiently polite time I managed to recline her onto the bed and wheel it back to ICU, by which time she was exhausted. Everyone had meant well but that was no solace for Julie, who was completely drained by the whole expedition. I left her closed-eyed and hopefully falling asleep, and will return about 9pm to check if all is well. At least she did see something other than the inside of ICU, which was the good doctor's intention, but was too weak to appreciate it.

Early Night

Julie's vitality level is not improving and is worse than two days ago. She needs food, yet she's too tired to eat. We are offering her soft, easily edible foods but yesterday's intake was insufficient. Omelette, tea, small amounts of fruit, a small cup of vegetable soup and some biscuits during the night. She has been in ICU for nearly two weeks, so it is becoming critical she has more nourishment. The hospital does provide a cup of milk mixed with protein-vitamin-mineral-chocolate powder. Tomorrow, I will experiment with curd-rice. I need to source high carbohydrate foods which are easily chewable. Her energy today was low, as has been the case for the last few days.

Psychologically, Julie is experiencing a few problems. Firstly, she is fed up with ICU but unless she shows signs of improvement they will be reluctant to move her. Secondly, she is exasperated with the oxygen tubes. A tube with two little inserts is placed into the nose, but her nostrils have become irritated so she throws it off immediately. The oxygen mask gets the same treatment. Dr. Shiva says that people always dislike the mask. She can breathe without extra oxygen but her saturation level is too low (around 85-87, when it should be in the high 90s). She is still using a urinary catheter, and I discussed the use of a bed-pan with the doctor, as well as the method I mentioned previously of her pivoting on her good leg to the commode. We shall see.

One problem is the lack of context for why she is in hospital. She accepts from me that she had a fall but there is a gap in continuity.

I am ready with numerous activities to rally her awareness but she requires the vigour to take these in. This morning I showed her photos of Trichy. The last memory she has is of leaving Thanjavur, so I'd have thought that Trichy photos, especially with her in them, were an easy way to jog memory. So far, she only has enough strength to look at very few photos on the computer. With improvement, I will call her friends on my phone – last night she even spoke with me over the phone from ICU. Progress reveals as the day advances.

The plan for tomorrow: look at photos whenever she is ready, a cup of milk with additives then tea or coffee and omelette. Post-lunch we tackle the toilet drama, and she rallies through self-interest at that point. Later, hopefully, curd-rice and biscuits. High-energy biscuits are not easy to find so I will trawl the market during the day. They are not a concept the locals would generally know about, though I have seen them in India.

Late Night

Julie's condition has become a serious concern for me, one reason being the lack of nourishment. I sit beside her in despair of how to get food into her. If she doesn't eat she will die, which I have told her. She understands but is too feeble to care. I succeeded in obtaining biscuits with added protein, vitamins and minerals, and she had a few of those just now. I also brought her a treat: a Mars bar. She had a couple of mouthfuls and liked that! She had tea and coffee during the day, finishing most of the omelette this morning, but ate almost none of the fried rice brought back from Vasanta Bhavan this evening.

I spoke with Dr. Baskaran, because it is hard to believe that lack of food alone is causing her condition to deteriorate. He said the main problem is the infection in her upper right lung. This sounds plausible. Energy is being consumed by this infection, leaving too little for mental alertness and appetite.

Meanwhile, my hands are improving – I was able to massage Julie's feet for the first time today. I still can't remove the top off my morning tea thermos, or the lid from drinking-water bottles. Opening doors is a challenge and I have developed a technique for each door I need to open through the day. Those obstacles are reducing but there is another difficulty: as I am trying to keep my hands dry, it means I can't wash them properly before and after eating or entering and leaving hospital. In ICU, alcohol hand-wash works well. I avoid using my hands for eating, relying on fork-and-spoon-foods only, as Indian food tends to be oily and difficult to clean from the fingers. It is essential not to carry an infection to Julie, or pick one up in the hospital, entailing a lot of planning and mindfulness.

Also, my sprained ankle doesn't allow me to have sufficient exercise. I can walk on it carefully for short distances but it aches from the knee down at night. I always walk to and from my favourite restaurant once or twice a day, for the physical activity as much as their great food. It is just the right distance for my foot to manage.

Sunday, February 9 (day 14)

Afternoon

I am despondent. Why is Julie so lethargic? I have my plans, with memory items and eating, but she remains so exhausted around midday that there is nothing we can do, and she has eaten no food. I succeeded in enticing her with half a cup of sweet coffee, and had to leave it at that.

Evening

Encouraging improvement during the afternoon: she had consumed most of the omelette, biscuits, two little bits of Mars bar, rest of the coffee, a cup of tea, some paneer fried rice, and a whole banana! I washed her teeth, finally worked the bed ratchet myself and shifted her back up the bed. I won't do that again as it opened up the wound in my right palm. And she had a small phone talk with Tony, her brother, in Australia.

I showed her photos of Trichy which she had taken before the accident. At first, she couldn't recall anything but then suddenly remembered. Following that, she recognised them all as we went through a number of photos. I showed her the book she had been reading, and she remembered that too.

Also, I was able to speak with Dr. Shiva. In between saving a man's life who was in the bed across from Julie, he found time to discuss her situation with me.

"She is stable," he said, "she can fly if you wish."

"But she can't sit up." I objected.

"No, she can't sit."

So that made it hopeless to imagine travelling on four flights but was promising news nonetheless. It is encouraging but I am under no illusions – despite this evening's uplift, her food intake remains insufficient and talk of travel irrelevant if her lung infection spreads, which is likely. Being so weak, she may not be able to fight this off.

Night

The infection is still the main concern. Consulting Dr. Shiva again, he repeated, "She has to do the breathing exercises to clear her lungs." Meanwhile, she is given new antibiotics. I expressed again the irritation she is having with ICU, and he agreed that she could move to a single room with a personal assistant. He'll confer with Dr. Baskaran. Julie, pleased to hear that, rallied to manage more breathing exercises this afternoon and evening, understanding why she has to do them. An x-ray tomorrow will show the degree of lung infection.

But she's depressed about her poor recovery. At a bad moment she uttered to me, "I'm losing it." Luckily, at that time I had just heard Dr. Shiva's assessment that she is held back by the lung condition, so could reassure her there was a reason for her weakness. Hopefully, it can be addressed.

Late Night

Back in my hotel room, distressed at the situation: it is obvious that the lung infection is critical. If it doesn't improve, all will be lost as Julie is in such a depleted condition this could easily finish her off. I have been conducting remote healing on her every night since the accident, even on the first evening when she was brought into ICU. Many others are also sending her healing in their own sincere ways. My online group has been working on this, as have Julie's friends on Facebook, where I have been posting numerous times a day to keep them informed and to have feedback from them.

I am continuously informed that here in Trichy there are Hindus at the temple, Muslims at the mosque, and Christians in church, all praying for Julie's recovery, as are many back in Australia. For years I have been using remote healing for her, and my efforts at this have always been effective at critical moments, so I settled into a dedicated session to heal her lung infection.

The Mysterious

My spontaneous visions of a massive feathered wing covering Julie has been mentioned. These visions have continued, which amazes me, as they haven't been instigated by my own volition. She had a dream in Langkawi at the beginning of our trip, wherein she was climbing an enormous structure, on top of which was a gigantic eagle. The eagle is the totem of Langkawi, and is sometimes depicted in folk-lore as Garuda. In fact, Langkawi was said to be one of Garuda's nesting sites. Garuda is the associated 'vehicle' of Vishnu. It is also coincidental that in our visit to Sri Ranganathaswamy Temple at Trichy, the day before the hotel fire, it was the shrine of Garuda which spontaneously opened before us as we stood in the pillared entrance area – another fascinating correlation. This brings me to an extraordinary instance of Julie's connections with the Gods of India.

Many examples could be related of the mysterious incidents Julie has experienced in India but one stood out for me when pondering this protective-wing vision. A major theme for us while travelling in India is Julie's health, and she becomes despairing when her body fails. While healthy, she has endless vitality and curiosity, as India is fabulous for curiosity. But when one is not well, India can revert to a nightmare.

She had had giardiasis in Varanasi, and the multiple antibiotics prescribed left her with mild diarrhoea, bloating and periodic tiredness. Although it was receding after considerable stress and difficulty, reoccurrence continued about every third or fourth day. Eventually, digestive enzymes and probiotics proved effective – an idea that dawned on me following another of my desperate healing efforts.

Julie had been distressed with her health issues while in Udupi, a holy town sacred to Krishna, an avatar of Vishnu, along the Konkan coast of Karnataka. One day we were watching the golden *ratha*, the procession cart, making the circuit on Car Road around the temples and *maths*, Hindu monasteries. The *murtis*, statues that embody the deities of Krishna and Radha, are brought out almost every evening in a procession with musicians, dancers, the temple elephant, fireworks and lights. Devotees obtain a good sighting – a darshan, blessing – of Krishna. This accessibility is a fundamental aspect of Krishna in Udupi, an important sacred city.

While watching the procession, looking at Krishna and feeling concerned for Julie's ailments, I asked Him to 'lift the veil' for her, to see the spirit of the Gods, as well as lifting the veil of her illness so she could carry on with the main purpose of this trip.

The following night we were at the temples again – it is an entrancing atmosphere. We decided to peek through the 'window' at Krishna. This is a famous aperture. The story tells that long ago an 'untouchable', a devotee not allowed into the temple to receive Krishna's darshan, was seated outside. Suddenly, the temple wall cracked open and the icon of Krishna turned, facing this wall fracture, to be seen by the man outside. It is said that this event changed the mood and ethos of the temple ever after. A window was made where the cleft had opened, and Krishna remained facing that direction. It is customary these days for devotees to gaze in through the window before entering the temple.

Krishna and Radha on the Golden Ratha at Udupi

A crowd had gathered at this window and I gave up waiting for my turn, but Julie, lingering patiently until everyone had left, gained a perfect view. Inside, a puja was proceeding with many devotees, as there would be no external cart procession that night. All at once the crowd parted leaving Julie a clear sighting of the ceremony. Priests were holding up a large cloth which they quickly withdrew at the crucial point of the puja, revealing the icon of Krishna directly in Julie's vision. A common theme in Hinduism is the drawing aside of the veil of *maya* to reveal God – the veil is the illusion of separateness.

Julie was thrilled to have glimpsed this sight. After that high point, we sat awhile on the seats beside Car Road absorbing the wonderful atmosphere of this place, then decided to depart for dinner. As we walked away from the temple area we were struck by the sight of two girls, twins about four years old, with identical laughing faces and thick, curly black hair. Amongst the evening lights they radiated merriness, playing near their mother at a street stall. Delighted, we stopped with pleasure, Julie especially being enchanted by these magical girls. The energy around them was truly vibrant and joyous. Their mother and her friends smiled at seeing us looking on (Julie gazes unashamedly!) The whole scene immediately became apparent to me: this was Krishna revealing himself to us in the flesh, vivifying these pretty young girls in their equally pretty little dresses. One of the representations of Vishnu is 'The Twins' – the legend of Nara-Narayana, Krishna-Arjuna.

I was spellbound with joy, as was Julie. The energy followed us into Woodlands restaurant, which was also in high spirits that night. Julie felt better physically and mentally in the days following.

So it was not without considerable history and repeated encouragement for my healing sessions, that I focused intently on the infected mucous lifting from her lungs, out of her body. I knew this was physically nearly impossible, as the only way to eliminate that blockage in the lungs is to cough it out, and that can take weeks, even for a healthy person. But I focused on visualising that clearing and healing, anyway. Afterwards, I went off to a deep sleep, exhausted again from a dramatic day.

Monday, February 10 (day 15)

Morning

An x-ray this morning revealed Julie's lung infection had almost completely gone! I was dumbstruck – how could that happen so quickly? There was still some phlegm but seeing the comparison x-rays, it was incredible how clear her right lung had become overnight. It also showed that the drainage tube had been pushed almost completely out of her left side, due to strong lung expansion. Thus, the doctors, themselves amazed, are planning to remove the remaining tubes today and if all goes well, move her to a single room tomorrow with twenty-four-hour attendance.

She has been sleeping most of the morning, having eaten only one bite of omelette and a cup of coffee. Being a Sunday, the physio didn't come today, so she escaped her morning torture session. I told her the good news about her lungs just now and she smiled. When she woke up later, she appeared considerably clearer. She keeps saying, "I've got to wake up." This statement stayed with me for a long time, as a compelling sign that deep inside, her awareness remained intact.

Afternoon

She is feeling more positive. Lifting of the infection has also lifted her mood. The target now is to build strength over the next week in preparation for flying. We are not in a position to be sure of the time frame yet, but it's good to have a target. If she rallies this afternoon and evening as she did yesterday, I will be more assured.

View from Vasanta Bhavan restaurant.
Taken on my last night in Trichy – market was quieter this night.

It has been strange how often my sister, Marilyn, calls me from Australia just as I am leaving the hospital on my way to the restaurant. As I walk through the crowded markets towards Vasanta Bhavan, dodging rickshaws and people, I am able to discuss the endless issues, and she keeps asking me how I am holding up while all this attention is focused on Julie. We finish the conversation as my food arrives. It's a pure coincidence but a support for me that she happens to ring at the right time.

I have identified the most propitious times to arrive at Vasanta Bhavan, as it can become busy. My favourite table overlooks the tank and market; often I am overwhelmed by the beauty and fascination of the scene below me. In these moments I almost pinch myself to see if I'm dreaming. I have longed to take photos and film but my hands are not capable of holding nor operating a camera. On every visit, the waiters inspect my hands for improvements, and ask "How is madam?" This is a great place for me to refuel my soul, along with a visit to the ground-level Shiva shrine of Rock Fort Temple on my return to the hospital.

Night

Tonight, Julie had a panic attack – in fact two. She was saying, "Get it off me! Get it off me!" I couldn't make the bloody nurses understand the words "panic attack" or even "sedative", which really pissed me off. I'd have thought it wouldn't be necessary to know English, or even to be a nurse, to recognise a panic attack. She suffered through the first one with just me, doing everything I could to reassure her safety. Julie knew exactly what was happening to her – she kept saying "panic attack". She nodded at my support but another side of her mind was unable to stop the fright.

Once the first trauma subsided, she smiled at me and understood what she had been through. We started on dinner – vegetable soup, biscuits and banana, but I could see the panic symptoms building again as we neared the end of the food interlude.

This time the nurse got the idea, and asked "Fear?" I said "Yes, ring the doctor!" The more experienced nurses were not on duty – they have the day off – so we only had the understudies. She did ring the doctor, who at least knew immediately what to do. Next, the nurse was giving Julie a sedative. She knew she needed a sedative, as when I was trying to communicate that to the nurse, she was nodding vigorously. When the medication was going into the CVC tube, she also understood, and was visibly relieved. Calming down, she went off to sleep.

The doctor thinks this incident is connected to her having been too long in ICU. I'm sure that is not helping but I sense there is more going on than only ICU. It is exactly two weeks to the night that Julie was admitted. And this is the first sign she has shown of a psychological reaction to the trauma. I suspect Marilyn is correct when she posited that the trauma is influencing Julie's energy, and tonight it surfaced. Is this a good thing, something that has to work its way out, or is it a sign of something she will have to deal with for a long time? Or both? Time will tell.

Hopefully, tomorrow they will move her out of ICU, and despite difficulties associated with that, at least it will be a change of scene. A window in the new room would be wonderful, if possible. The doctors keep saying there will be 24hour assistance, but at what level of skill?

Late Night

There's never a dull moment with this woman. I've been called back to the hospital twice tonight, but not for panic attacks. That's over, and now she's into obstructionist mode. She won't let them do anything to her. The first time, she wouldn't let the cleaning women clean her up from what they call 'passing a motion'. I intervened to obtain her cooperation but she is becoming stubborn.

Next call: returning again, I had to assist the nurses in attending to various details like giving her pills, helping put the new bottle into her CVC tube, and she watches them like a hawk. She even tried to bite one of the nurses for trying to put the gadget on her finger that reads the oxygen saturation level. I told them to leave it, and put it on when she's asleep, if they must. She became restless. The message is clear – she's fed up with the whole ICU scene, and doesn't want any more of it.

And physically, she's right. I even saw her turn onto her left, broken ribs side, twice without pain. A few times, earlier, she did have pain, but after that it didn't bother her. I believe she's strong enough to get up and walk around. I'm glad I haven't given her any more Mars bar, or she would have jumped the rails. I see a pattern, with her going through emotional moods in an unstable way. It is probably part of her psychological healing process, but she will definitely have to be moved out of ICU tomorrow. She's made sure of that!

Julie's mental recovery progresses, yet has a long way to go. Remaining so long in ICU has not helped, not that it could have been avoided. She has periods of greater clarity but often mixes things up or loses track of the situation. Considering that she is in a place where the lights shine relentlessly, beeping sounds continue constantly, the nurses are poking at things on and around her, she can't control her own toileting, and she hasn't the energy to even hold up a book, to say nothing of the continual medications being administered, it is understandable how all this is working against her mental recovery.

Return to Australia Considerations

I am talking regularly with the insurance people and the Australian Consul. Discerning the best way to transport Julie back to Australia has been exercising my mind, and I have had numerous discussions with those who handle our case for the insurance company. They are a case manager, astute with the overall details, and the medical 'team' – a nurse who helps me navigate the medical technicalities. Both are helpful and responsive.

The insurance company will pay for and organise the return flights as long as we agree, which we do so far – the principle being that Julie's health comes first. Lying down or extended reclining is available in business class, but not all our flights have business class or extended reclining. It is possible to transport fully supine passengers in emergencies, but Julie is close to being able to sit. What is required is sufficient health for her to sit on the smaller flights and recline on the longer ones. It is important that the lung infection is fully healed and her oxygen levels are high, before flying.

We will require four flights: Trichy to Chennai, Chennai to Singapore, Singapore to Sydney, Sydney to Armidale. This will mean staying one or two nights between flights for recovery. The whole operation will necessitate her being in considerably better shape than she is at present. There are direct Trichy to Singapore flights but they don't have business class, and the flight is over four hours. The best flight plan is with Singapore Airlines, who operate a business class from Chennai – Singapore – Sydney. The Trichy to Chennai flight remains a 'sitting' one, so she will need to be fit for that.

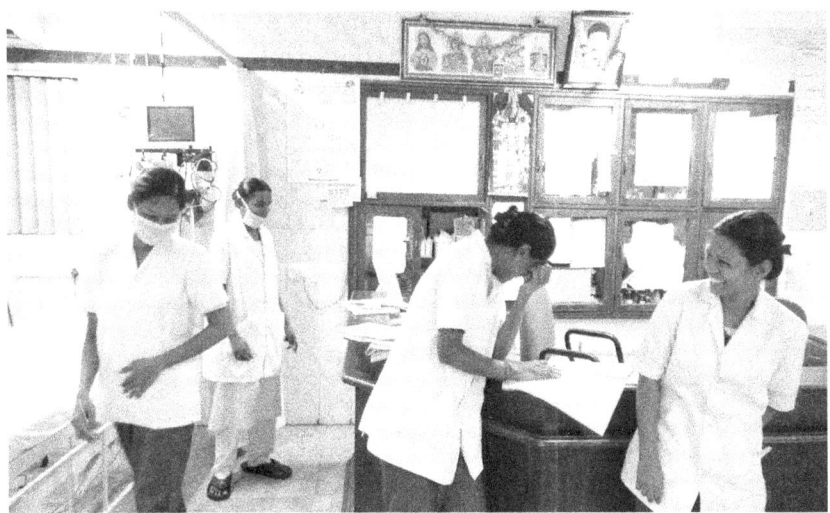

Julie's ICU bed (left) and nurses (Mythili on the left, Kothai on right)

GVN Medical Ward

Tuesday, February 11 (day 16)

Morning

I was convinced that Julie's actual physical capacity was stronger than fatigue was allowing her to utilise. I spoke with Dr. Baskaran this morning about this, and he said, "Let's try it."

Despite her usual morning grogginess, we sat her up on the bed edge, and then to standing. She handled that well, so a chair was brought and she sat down. She wasn't happy but also not in pain. She sat there for about half an hour, while eating a biscuit and banana. Once she had definitely had enough, she was transferred out of ICU, downstairs to the second floor, and into a single room which is around the corner from the main corridor. It is quieter but without a view of the Neem tree. I suppose you can't have quietness *and* tree.

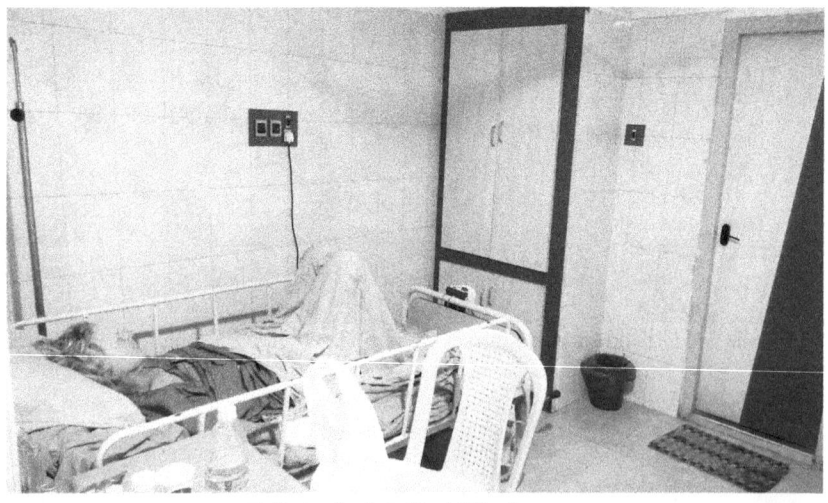

Julie in the Medical Ward room

More good news is that Mythili is allocated to be her dedicated assistant. She, at least, knows what a panic attack is! So things are progressing. The doctor told me that Julie is on three antibiotics, one of which he will cease today.

The discussion with Dr. Baskaran turned to return-flight matters. It is good to canvas the likely problems and solutions with him. We have to see how Julie adapts over the next few days before serious plans can be made, including advice from the medical experts. Physical, psychological and energetic risks have to be factored in with every possible situation covered. Naturally, her being in general good shape will be the best preparation.

Afternoon

This drama never ends. I am now in the single room with Julie. 'Twenty-four hour assistance' actually means only twelve hours. I will sleep here with her tonight, and possibly for the next week. There is an extra 'cot', a padded bench which I'll find a way to make comfortable. It is important that Julie has someone familiar to accompany her through the night, except presumably, she will be asleep! Hopefully, I will be too. The air conditioner though, is right above my bed. To keep the room cool for Julie on the opposite side it will mean a cold night for me.

She still hasn't reverted to herself fully. I have requested speaking with the psychiatrist to see what he can offer by way of explaining what she is going through, but it's probably merely a matter of time. Optimistically, in a few days she can sit at the little desk they have provided and use her laptop.

What is not helping is that she has antibiotic-induced mild diarrhoea. To ameliorate that condition I have given her probiotics and a little loperamide. Dr. Baskaran thinks she only needs curd, which I am giving, but this diarrhoea causes such drama that some respite from the basic bodily troubles will be a blessing. In this hospital there is a requirement for relatives to maintain the supporting tasks. My capacity in this is limited but at least I can ensure her basic needs are attended.

Physically, there is a little improvement. She sat up again for some time, so that aspect continues to progress. It's a case of finding solutions to every new problem that arises.

Evening

Fran's 'second-attempt' roses arrived! Julie was delighted.

I have been worried about Julie's mental state. Tonight she was moaning and twisting in pain, talking about wanting to go to the toilet, even though she had just been earlier. I don't know why the temporary remedy hadn't dawned on me sooner. The antibiotics were causing problems in her intestinal tract, which was considered normal, but it hadn't occurred to me to give her a simple paracetamol tablet.

Half an hour after taking paracetamol, she was talking to me normally. It was so satisfying. It had only been the pain in her guts that was making her spin out. We talked about Fran's choice of flowers, about her Facebook friends, and how strange the whole thing has been.

I walk to the hotel after giving Julie dinner (when she eats). In my hotel room I update her friends on Facebook, change into rough clothes, collect what is required for the night and return to the hospital. Following that, we wait until the nurses and doctors have finished, which is often past midnight, then settle down to sleep. During the night Julie occasionally wakes in pain or moaning about something. There is little I can do except give her paracetamol if sufficient time has passed since the last dose. The nights are always broken by some drama – I don't get much sleep.

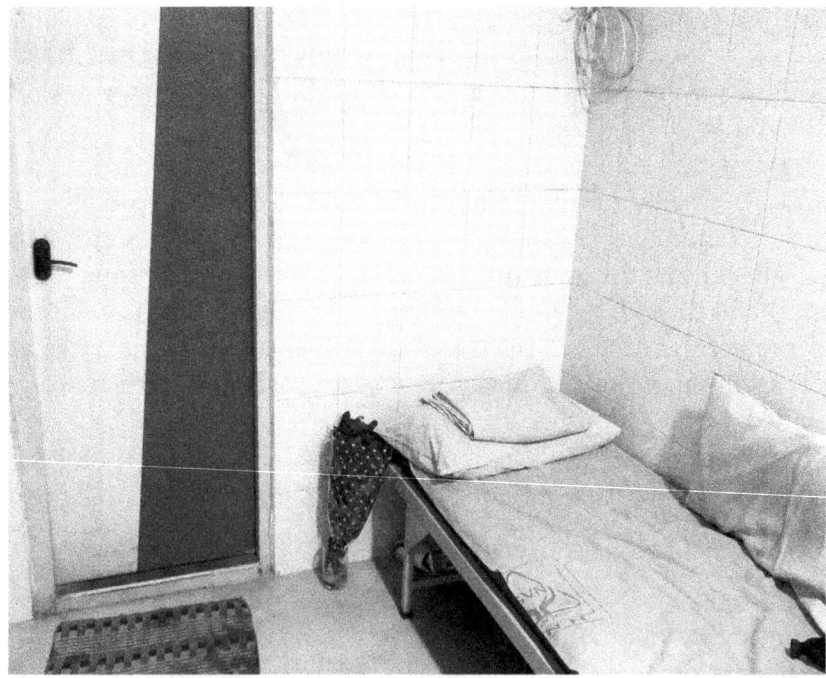

Michael's bed, toilet door which Julie watches constantly, and Fran's flowers

Wednesday, February 12 (day 17)

Morning

After about three hours sleep last night, I returned to the hotel and managed another half-hour. I'm glad I had been with Julie during the night as difficulties arose. She looks better this morning, and she should have more rest through the day.

She's taken to saying "Mind you.." She will be in the midst of groaning about her gut pains then say, "Mind you.." sometimes even making an astute reflection, though mostly to say she wants to go to the toilet.

One of Julie's Facebook friends recommended onion, so I arranged to have onion cooked with her morning omelette, prepared by the hospital canteen. The doctors are not keen on including the yolk in her omelette, due to health concerns about eggs in India. Just now, the nurses are busy attending to her drainage tube. They may also remove her central venous catheter, because not only has it been in one place for some time, but last night she was fiddling with it unconsciously. This means it must be itching. It could be a real emergency if she pulled that out.

Currently, her main difficulties are the constant abdominal pains and diarrhoea from antibiotics. To resolve this I gave her one loperamide last night, which has not blocked her up, and one this morning. Mindful of her normal dose for loperamide, I'm keeping it lower, to be safe. Then there are digestive enzymes which she found helpful following the last antibiotic episode in Varanasi, and probiotics, as well as curd (yoghurt) three times a day if possible. I've tried to avoid sugar and instead use honey in tea and curd. The nurses are administering medication for bowel pains, so hopefully she will recover from this condition because it is the main factor restraining her normal state of mind.

I discussed possible travel options with Dr. Senthil, who said he will confer with the other doctors on Julie's case tomorrow. Without setbacks, her recovery expectations should allow us to target leaving in about eight days time. Every day provides a better time frame. I don't want to jump prematurely but our visas run out on February 21st, and we may require a day in Chennai between flights. Dr. Senthil is adamant Julie does not sit in a chair or wheelchair for some days, as he explains that if the fracture in her left hip becomes aggravated it will entail major surgery. Currently, it is healing without her awareness of problems. She is able to easily sit up in bed with assistance now, so that is good. Hopefully, she will begin reading later today but she won't be interested if her colic pains continue.

Afternoon

What bothers me is Dr. Senthil's advice for her to not sit in a chair, or walk. For exactly how long, I'm not sure. This has caused concerns about our time frame for departure. As Marilyn has pointed out, there is a lot of sitting on aeroplanes regardless of reclining seats. But more than that, Julie will need to use the toilets on the plane, in the airport, at hotels and so forth.

The best prospect would be if she is capable of walking for short distances, albeit with assistance, and to sit for at least an hour in seats that are not too upright, nor have the type of padding which causes the pelvis to fold in slightly. For these situations, she will need sufficient time, after clearance by doctors that it is safe to begin exercises. The alternative is to require considerably more assistance and increased risk. Dr. Senthil thinks that a wheelchair with assistance would be enough, and in some places, as in Singapore and Sydney, we can probably use wheelchair taxis. Nonetheless, Julie will need to sustain reasonable sitting expectations, even if not ultimately necessary. She will prefer that, being particularly resistant to fuss made about her movements – having always been like that and not as yet adversely affected.

It appears that sitting should be a prerequisite to departure. Going to the toilet on the plane is probably the most difficult scenario. I have to think this through and get advice from doctors, the insurance medical team and their travel agents.

The Australian Consul is able to assist in visa extensions, which require online application. They have sent me the Web link. I will wait until I have spoken with doctors and the insurance medical team, but if staying extra time is advisable, we will do that. Hopefully, it won't be for too long.

Night

The psychiatrist came. I wanted to consult about what to expect in Julie's trauma situation, but he came too late at night for that discussion. Anyway, after examining her, he said she was suffering from stress and a stress-related gastric ulcer which causes the pain. He prescribed mild calmatives for her, and something else which I didn't catch (three pills).

I had been futilely searching the local area in the last two days for a Himalayan Herbs shop, to purchase herbal calmatives. There was a great shop with many such items but it was all in Tamil, and no one to help. So, I was pleased he prescribed calmatives because it was obvious Julie required something to help her relax. Unfortunately, these guys have a habit of going to excess, though he presents as an intelligent person. We will see how this works.

Regarding gastric ulcers: whatever they call it and its cause, she possibly has something like that, so I should now be thinking of best and worst foods for gastric ulcers.

My Condition

Today, I was reaching my limits – nearly collapsed on the walkway through the market in a heap of tears. I have been pushing on through all obstacles, day and night, for so long, and still not recovered from the fire trauma. A wave of emotional exhaustion flooded me as, with my injured ankle, I carefully picked my way among the broken roadway rocks and rubble. About to collapse crying, I caught myself and realised this condition must be remedied. It was no use me falling apart with Julie needing constant assistance.

This was not the first time I had felt this wave. Over the last two weeks I've felt it growing, and ignored it, but it couldn't be disregarded any more. I asked my private healing group to send healing energy and, being a practical person, dug out the multivitamins and minerals from our travelling medicine bag.

Too often I assume indestructibility, because in general that's been my life experience This event has thrust me to the brink of exhaustion in a strange way. Obviously, a lot of traumatic stress from this incident will need releasing to keep functioning optimally. Not knowing how long this saga will continue, I had best prepare for the long haul and measure my energy.

Thursday, February 13 (day 18)

Morning

Much better sleep last night, despite being in a hospital. Whatever the psychiatrist gave Julie has certainly helped her sleep.

I conferred with Dr. Senthil again. He wants Julie to remain in bed for six weeks from her fall, for adequate repairing of wrist and pelvis fractures. They will x-ray again at four weeks from operation, meaning a week-and-a-half's time, to determine bone-fixing progress. To begin preparations for departure, I could possibly push them to have this checked sooner. That's not totally irresponsible as I am familiar with

Julie's healing potential, and another doctor here thinks she should be moving from bed to commode sooner. But Dr. Senthil is the boss and the orthopaedic expert, so his word goes. Let's see how x-rays look over the next week or more but I am definitely now looking at staying as long as necessary.

The problem is, staying that length of time at this hospital is going to drive Julie mad, which is not wise for her mental recovery. It is not wise for me either: need to be careful I don't crack up. I sent off an email to the insurance case manager, copying in the Australian Consul, detailing these issues about Julie's recovery, and one of their medical team rang me while she was in for chest x-ray.

Nothing can be done until the haemothorax, the leaking of fluid from her left rib fractures, clears up, which I thought it had, but apparently not. This measure is sensible – she needs hospital care while that aspect is healing – but after, there is no good reason for her to stay in hospital. It's only a matter of having her toileting and food requirements supported until they give the go-ahead to begin leg and chair movements. In Western countries, there are rehabilitation places for this kind of care, so I asked the insurance medial team to investigate what can be done here in Trichy. Even a hotel with a trained personal assistant would work, so long as it's wheelchair friendly and with Julie's preferred diet. It's also possible she could travel by ambulance to a retreat not too far.

Speaking by phone today with her brother, Tony, she said, "I feel like I've been captured by bandits."

Regarding the gastric ulcer controversy: at this point there are no alternative theories and the doctors consider it as a minor issue, which will clear up without treatment. Most likely this is antibiotic related, as examinations by the gastroenterologist indicates there are no internal injuries. It hasn't flared again but another related symptom is the constant feeling she needs to visit the toilet. There must be bowel cramping involved – I will mention this to a doctor but I'm not expecting much interest.

Afternoon

This toilet obsession is wearing me down. She keeps thumping her plastered right arm on the bed rail, demanding to use the toilet. She can see the toilet room door when I open it for myself, and knows what's in there! I explain over and over that she can't go to the toilet, that she has to do it in her diaper, but it doesn't sink in. I find it exhausting. She is aware enough to engage and wants me to help her use the toilet, but can't retain my explanations of why she is not allowed out of bed. Sometimes I just have to leave, escaping from the endless repetition, only to return an hour later to exactly the same routine. When she is like this there is no intelligent communication between us. I find that difficult to sustain for any length of time, especially as I have nothing with which to occupy myself when I'm with her.

My hands are still covered in scabs. To pass the time I fiddle with the scabs as they itch, and small sections break off. Completely unaware of my injuries (unless I show them to her, at which she become concerned for as long as her attention holds), Julie says to me, "Playing with your pretty little hands again?" But mostly all she says is, "I want to do a poo!" She is surprisingly conscious of everything around her, and at the same time obsessed with her bowel problems. It is a curious and often funny mix. She can be creative in her comments.

These are both symptoms of her brain injury condition but I had only instinctive comprehension of that at this point. I wish the psychiatrist had been more informed of this syndrome, but alas, Julie and I were completely in the dark about it for a long time.

Night

Julie's chest drain-tube has been removed, finally! That's the last tube in her, aside from the bladder catheter. One less infection risk.

The psychiatrist came in around midnight, and I explained to him about her bowel cramping. He prescribed something to alleviate that – let's hope it works. If the cramps are gone by tomorrow, we should be able to move to better eating and other interesting things. Even though she is in pain, she is still more her normal self than previously. I gave her a paracetamol finally for the night, which calmed her down.

We certainly won't be moving from this hospital for at least a week to ten days. It's for the one to two weeks following I am considering an alternative location. It will need to be a supportive facility. I don't intend being the only carer just to be out of hospital. That would be senseless.

Friday, February 14 (day 19)

Morning

At 1am last night, in came a nurse all bright and cheery, turned on the lights, woke Julie up and asked if she wanted a cup of tea or coffee! In the most restrained way possible, we finally persuaded her to leave. It was not a good night's sleep.

The last two days Julie has had colic pains of one sort or another, which made her unwilling to eat or engage. Today, there are no pains but she is zonked-out. I suspect they gave her excess of some medication and I will see the psychiatrist about that tonight. She has tried to eat, although not enough. Still, it was better than yesterday.

Late Morning

Big surprise! There was a knock at the door, which we always try to have closed to keep the noise down, and to restrict totally unrelated people wandering in to gawk at us. On opening the door, my mind couldn't register what presented. There were two Western people saying "Hello". There are few Westerners in Trichy, and none in the hospital, but these people seemed to know us! In fact, it was Julie's dentist from Australia, Cristy Norton, and a friend of hers, Paul.

When my mind finally overcame the impossibility of the situation, we discovered Cristy and Paul were part of a volunteer group touring medical establishments around the Trichy area in Tamil Nadu. They had been visiting ICU upstairs when they were told two Australians were in the hospital. It didn't take them long to realise who we were, and they turned up with various goodies. Julie was wonderfully surprised and delighted to see them. Their guide, Ramu, gave me good information and contacts, about obtaining non-vegetarian food of high quality from the Hotel Sangam.

One item they gave us was a big tube of Vegemite. I was able to pull apart a terrible sandwich just thrown away in disgust, add the Vegemite, and with a little reconstruction Julie had a delicious and healthy extra for lunch. She is less dopey than yesterday but still 'written-off', as she calls exhaustion.

Afternoon

Meanwhile, aside from dealing with visa matters, I have visited two other large hospitals. A curious thing about pronunciations: it is so difficult to get them right as the following example illustrates. I was informed of a hospital called 'Kempsey' which, when I told the rickshaw driver, he knew immediately. At the hospital to which I was delivered, I couldn't find any name like Kempsey – it was called Kauvery. I asked, and finally a doctor understood – he said the hospital was called 'KMC' (Kauvery Medical Centre). Now, if I had asked the rickshaw driver for KMC he would not have a clue what I meant!

I have also been to the Apollo Hospital, some distance out along the road to Thanjavur. The idea behind this is to establish Julie in a good room in a main hospital, more comfortable than GVN. It must be as close as possible to a hotel room for me, and with the required medical support. Both hospitals looked fine. The Apollo has a bigger TV and generally everything new, albeit sterile. The other, KMC, looked suitable, and it was also in the cantonment area of the city, a Westerner-friendly area. By comparison, Apollo is way out on the highway, miles from anywhere. At KMC I would be able to augment Julie's menu with items sourced from outside, especially non-vegetarian food. That is the clincher, as well as being more interesting for me.

I will consult with the insurance people tomorrow but doubt she will be ready to move for a few days. With the chest drain removed, there is nothing medical remaining for the GVN doctors to complete.

Saturday, February 15 (day 20)

I conducted an initial reconnaissance tonight of the big Hotel Sangam that Cristy, Paul and Ramu recommended. By auto-rickshaw it is approximately a half-hour trip across the city. Once there, Ramu's contact introduced me to his friend the restaurant manager. I returned to our little sparse hospital room with Chicken Maryland, Hawaiian Chicken Salad, cooked, battered bananas and pineapple. It was yummy! Julie gobbled it up. A last, I've found something with which her taste buds can override her tiredness. Hopefully, she didn't eat too much.

Of three things that I know well by this age, the third is travelling in India. I've been doing this for forty years, and by now, very little doesn't constantly surprise me. But this current drama has pushed and astounded me to my limits. The trip to the hotel was no exception. A prissy French tour group were supping their delicate dinners in fine style, local plump politicians pomped around in their puffy, characteristic way, while gun-toting military and police guards filled the foyer in their bemused manner (there was an election happening). Dozens of horrific near-misses occurred on the rickshaw rides, impoverished people listlessly crept along road sides, sadhus set up actually *right on* the busy road, and I found myself nearly crying over a beer in the restaurant – I might have to give the beer a swerve. At home in Australia, weeks pass with little change, while here, every minute is chaos. It's so hard not to hate and love this place in equal measure.

Something has been annoying the hell out of me for days, and consuming a huge amount of my energy and time – my computer failed to start after a Windows Update. I have been trying everything I know to fix this problem but it beats me at every turn. You can't believe how maddening it is when each carefully prepared recovery strategy is thwarted by an unexpected block. Finally, tonight I hit upon a simple and effective trick. I have been able to get into the second Operating System on the machine, and subsequent to research on the Web, simply replaced a few boot files with those from the good Operating System. It worked! Unbelievable reprieve. The last thing I need in this situation is for my computer to clap out. But until I can repair the recovery mechanisms, it will remain vulnerable.

Sunday, February 16 (day 21)

Morning

I spoke with Dr. Senthil: the insurance agents had been in contact with him yesterday, so we discussed my relocation concerns for Julie's recovery. He explained that if she was moved to KMC hospital, his continuation of treatment would not be possible. This is a good point, as although a second opinion on her orthopaedic status would be useful, I am well satisfied with his treatment, as I am with the quality of all the doctors at GVN. He suggested instead, that I consider ABC hospital, where he would be able to continue his management of Julie's progress.

On the second attempt, this evening, I was able to look at ABC's room and talk with the directing doctor, who is a friend of Dr. Senthil. The room was perfectly suitable, in fact perhaps even better than the other large hospitals. There was a problem about the food, in that it is a vegetarian-only hospital (they all are in Trichy) and they weren't keen on my bringing in non-vegetarian meals from outside, but in the end I prevailed – that should be fine.

So that is satisfactory, and I have discussed ABC hospital with the insurance case manager. They will need to do their processes before a shift, which means the room I looked at will be taken. But they have rooms coming available all the time, so it shouldn't be a problem as long as the next vacant one, when we are ready, is equally suitable.

Evening

Julie was sedated again today, but Dr. Senthil and another doctor agreed they should completely phase out sedatives over the next two days.

I went to the Hotel Sangam again to obtain dinner, and there met Cristy, Paul and their whole gang. They graciously paid for our dinner, and handed over a large bag of goodies, including muesli! They were very friendly, and gave me a beer and good advice from a physio in the group. It was a real pleasure to be with them. But, as always at the Hotel Sangam, I find it distressing to be in such a refined and trouble-free environment, knowing that Julie is lying on a primitive hospital bed in a spartan room back through the swamp of traffic across town, waiting for me. The contradictions cause intense emotions to surface that, along with the traffic dangers involved, I find myself dreading these trips to the Hotel Sangam. Yet at the same time, am extremely grateful to have found it.

Night

Julie loved the food, and went off to sleep with a happy tummy. I approached Dr. Baskaran regarding the ridiculous business of doing things to Julie so late at night and early in the morning. How is anyone to get enough sleep in this place? That conversation has worked, and tonight they dispensed her last medications before 10pm. Mythili, as usual, came down from ICU especially to administer these. It's always a pleasure to see her. She is so competent and gentle.

I thought Julie would be walking soon. God knows she wants to. But as the time lengthens with each new piece of orthopaedic information, I need to evaluate alternatives. One issue is how Julie could travel by aeroplane if she returned to Australia before she can walk? I have discovered that we can travel business class all the way from Trichy to Sydney. That only leaves the last leg of the journey: Sydney to Armidale. Returning by ship has been suggested to me, and it does appear a possibility but perhaps an outside one. I will have to put these questions to the insurance medical team.

Our return date is stretching out further. Dr. Senthil would like to see Julie not stand (weight-bear) for another three weeks, but it will take some time before she can perform tasks like walking to, and using an in-flight toilet. A few days? One week? Two weeks? Add to that a few stopover days, and we are starting to creep well into the second half of March. The alternative is to fly with a catheter and diaper, which is not an attractive option. Hopefully, her fracture heals sooner, and she can start walking. But we can't be sure that will happen. I'll need to prepare for departure somewhere around the 22nd March.

Currently we are waiting until Monday to see what can be done about the other hospital, ABC. It has nice rooms, or at least the one I saw was, though there may be insurance issues. CHUBB, the insurance underwriter, works through an Indian insurance company, but do they have 'relations' with ABC hospital? There is much to do; but for the present, I would like to see Julie becoming more herself. Supposedly, her sedative dose was reduced today, and perhaps it has been, though now she has constipation. One thing after another keeps obstructing her normalisation, yet I'm convinced she is growing stronger behind these veils.

Tomorrow, I must try again to extend our visa. My first attempt today was futile. After going to several buildings beside the highway on the far side of the city, I arrived in the wrong place: the 'rural', not the 'urban' office for visa extensions. On Wednesday, the woman from the Australian Consulate in Chennai is flying here to visit us.

Monday, February 17 (day 22)

Morning

Julie and I discussed the departure plans last night. In principle, we would prefer to wait until she is fit enough, both to walk and to enjoy herself on the trip, though I continue to research the implications of an earlier return, which may become necessary. This will mean we won't be returning until late March. The necessary actions to anticipate this must be undertaken, as it extends our previous schedule: there are many things back in Australia as well as here in India that would be affected.

We both slept well, and feel better now to address all the little obstacles around the modified departure scenarios. Dr. Baskaran has agreed to instruct the nurses to complete night medications early and not wake us until after 7am. The only staff who remain a law unto themselves are the cleaning women. I'm sure they would do as they are told, but they are so far down the hierarchy that no one considers it appropriate for their status to even include these women. And we need their good relations, as they do the diaper cleaning. When this is done, I like to be present to confirm that everything is conducted correctly, and ensure sufficient supplies of the necessary items (often there aren't), like spare sheets and talc powder. Julie is developing a rash from this style of cleanup, which can never be effective. I also check that they roll her onto her right side, instead of the left which has the broken ribs. She is likely to just do what they say, and discover the pain when it's too late.

One of Julie's few memories from this time is of two of these cleaning women, in their distinctive blue and red saris, standing at the base of her bed chortling away to each other. They are no doubt 'untouchables', and don't have to uphold pretences. One I like but the other is lazy and grumpy; an eye has to be kept on her that she doesn't skimp on the job.

The main problem for Julie, aside from this constipation bout which is probably more about hospitalization than anything else, is that she is still on a half dose of anti-anxiety medication. I had spoken with two of her doctors, and they agreed to have that reduced or cut but it hasn't happened. Meaning, another day of el-zonko for her. I will speak more firmly to them this morning to have her taken off that treatment. There was a need following her panic attacks but that was over a week ago. She wants to engage with life now, as best she can.

Afternoon

I've just completed an extended consultation with the insurance team. The situation appears to be this:

Firstly, at what point can Julie fly, considering the implications of her chest condition? This is possibly two weeks after the drain tube is removed, which happened Friday night.

Secondly, at what point can she safely sit in a wheel chair with her pelvis fracture? The fracture is in the cup, so aggravation could mean a hip replacement – to be avoided at all cost. Would this be two weeks away also? Most likely longer, but possibly not as long as the month I am currently considering.

The Indian insurance company does not have existing 'relations' with ABC hospital: that will take a few days to set up. Thus, there will be no change of location for some days, if at all.

Tuesday, February 18 (day 23)

My condition

Since the climactic fire incident, I have been operating at a maintenance level of vitality. For some days I could not even eat, but when I recovered sufficiently to negotiate the details of my own situation, and respond effectively to Julie's ongoing needs, I remained at a barely functional capacity. I'm sure much of this was due to the shock, but also the whole event severely depleted my resources. To do anything, including managing my cleaning, clothes and nourishment, presented as huge obstacles that had to be surmounted with considerable tenacity.

Those tasks, and attending to Julie's roller-coaster of medical crises, consumed my available reserves of strength, so that when I had to research alternative hospitals, it confronted me like a sheer cliff to be scaled. It took an immense effort to engage with these external tasks, which under normal conditions, I would have found easy and exciting. It was as if I was constantly dragging my body, moving in a semi-trance of exhaustion.

When I began dealing with the official Indian bureaucracy, this sense of struggling through mud intensified. I never knew how I accomplished each of these tasks and excursions – I adopted the mode of one step in front of another, and somehow found the connections required in each case, progressing from one to another in a fatigued dream-state.

People in normal healthy fitness can rarely empathise with those for whom simply getting out of bed in the morning is a mammoth assault on the soul. This enervated condition took about a year to recede but fortunately I was familiar with it, as I had experienced a similar and more serious malaise in my late twenties which took ten years to repair. Nonetheless, the dealings with visas, banks, government agencies and police in Trichy at this time, demanded a fierce resolve to negotiate. So, although I describe each phase of the processes, through it all I was barely able to function, sustaining an effective mask throughout as a tightrope to cling to while dangling over an abyss of despair.

Morning

While Julie has been in an unresponsive state again today, I have dealt with the visa extension business: filling online forms, printing, and taking them to the Commissioner of Police headquarters, which is far away on the outskirts of the other side of town. At least I found the appropriate place first time today. Weirdly, it was the same location where I was incorrectly dropped off on the last foray, except I didn't realise then that it was, in fact, the right place: the 'urban' office. The police clerks were helpful and informed about the case. Sitting in their office for some time while they collected papers and made frustrating phone calls, most of which were non-connections, I was finally presented with a list of tasks which had to be completed *by tomorrow*, or we risked being fined for overstaying our visas!

Mani and Sathish at the hotel helped with some of the details, like obtaining a Treasury challan. This, I discovered, is a financial instrument for payments to the government. After considerable trouble with the hotel printer, involving a joint troubleshooting effort, the required forms were printed. At the hospital, Dr. Senthil has done his part, with a letter certifying Julie's condition. Tomorrow morning I must find where to pay the fee, trusting the hotel have printed the forms correctly (two of which were not). Fingers crossed! Tomorrow will be another busy day, meaning less time with Julie. Also, I have an intermittent cough which may have resulted from the traffic fumes.

Julie overcame her constipation on being sat up this morning, so that's the trick in future. As an exercise she is supposed to sit up in bed, and then on the edge of the bed – that's the limit. She can manage this when not fatigued. After speaking again (and again) with Dr. Baskaran this evening, he told the nurses to cease the anti-psychotic medication. 'Anti-psychotic'! So, the psychiatrist has been prescribing anti-psychotic medication. I hadn't realised. God knows if that was a help or not, but days of semi-coma don't look efficacious to me. I had suspected these psychiatrists weren't to be trusted, as all I had wanted was a conversation regarding what to expect from her trauma. Instead, they have to do their diagnosis and prescription ritual, without consulting me.

There will be no moving hospital to ABC for two or more days. The new place is not far away but in a different area. It has a long street nearby with many interesting shops to explore during my 'time out'. The shopkeepers there won't be asking me "How is madam?" and wanting to look at my hands (which are healing well), nor will I enjoy the assistance of the ever-helpful hotel staff and management. But a change will be welcome.

This morning I photographed the room we were in during the fire, and the view from the window, to show Julie one day if we make it back to Australia. I'll also take photos of the ICU and staff. Mythili has finally opened her Gmail account, so we will be able to keep in touch – Julie is keen to not lose contact with her.

I went to the Hotel Sangam again tonight for tasty dishes, which Julie enjoyed. Little by little, we are advancing. I am feeling better, even with the bureaucratic dramas.

Hospital Switch issue

The primary reason for changing hospitals is Julie's mental recovery. The room she is in currently is basic. It is small, and the bed is too short – we have to continuously keep pulling her back. It is insufficient in size and security for me to live in, requiring constant shifts between hotel and hospital. As we are anticipating a maximum of six more weeks in hospital, three of which, at least, confined to bed, she should be more comfortable.

The room in ABC Hospital had a good size modern hospital bed, a sitting area with couches and coffee-table, a reasonably sized bed for me, a TV and sufficient room to store our luggage so that I can move there from the hotel. These rooms, in fact all that I have seen in the hospitals I have looked at, have no windows. ABC's bathroom has a slight incline, but that should not matter greatly as Julie will be using a commode for the first period in which she is allowed out of bed for toileting. After that, the short incline will be good exercise.

As it is a larger hospital, it has a wide range of specialised support. Although not as big as KMC, there are advantages to a medium sized hospital over a huge one. ABC should be a good compromise – it is more up-market than GVN. The insurance medical team have reported on the hospital regarding recovery suitability, and they are satisfied. The down-side is that we will need to renegotiate the details of Julie's condition. It takes a while to address the myriad little issues, and the key people, but we have a reasonable amount of time for that. Also, sadly, we will be leaving the staff of GVN, though actually it's only Mythili that Julie will miss, and we can keep in touch with her.

To be honest, the recovery services are only an added bonus, as it is the room facilities that would be preferable for an extended stay. The real advantage of ABC over the others is the continued treatment by Dr. Senthil, in whom I have confidence. Continuity of treatment matters, as he knows the full history of her condition.

Late Afternoon, Visa Dramas

I'm completely exhausted, after dancing the visa extension jig all over Trichy. First stop was GVN Hospital, to collect the medical certificate and letter, which didn't mention me and had Julie's name wrong, so that had to be adjusted. Next, I organised the documents from the hotel, including verification of my residence. The hotel staff were extremely helpful in printing out multiple copies of the documents, once they got the printer working again, in case they were required (which they weren't).

Then I set off with money and documents. Initially, an auto-rickshaw took me to the State Bank of India, Main Office, to pay the fee by challan. Walking in through the front door there were counters lined up on both sides of a large hall. I wandered along until I identified someone to ask directions. "You are in the wrong place", he said. I was not surprised, as this confusion is always to be expected in India. Around the corner, down the path, and in through a little doorway ... I eventually located the right place, with a long line of people waiting to be served. Again, I wandered along until I found someone to ask. This was the right place! But the challan was not correctly registered and stamped! That must be done at the Treasury. Where was the Treasury?

"At the Collectors Office." And furthermore, I had to return within two hours with the correctly stamped challan, or that desk in the bank would be closed for the afternoon...

Right, time was against me now, without a clue where the Collectors Office was or how to get there. A man who overheard our conversation offered a ride on the back of his motorbike but I judged a rickshaw would be safer. So, now to find one with a driver who knew what the Collectors Office was, and how to get there. Fortunately, I discovered a rickshaw driver who seemed to know, although he did stop a few times asking for directions. Eventually, he dropped me at the Collectors Office, which, predictably, was not the location for the Treasury. "Around back-side" the guard wearily said. I walked around the back, across a lawn, through a hedge and along an old dirt road to a dilapidated building which, to my surprise, was the Treasury! Inside a corridor was a throng of men pushing their challans towards a single unperturbed woman behind a computer. It was a case of whoever could shove their challan in first would be served. Luckily, this woman was efficient and, with some helpful advice and not a little elbowing, I passed my challan to her. It wasn't long before she had it registered.

Next, so I was informed, it had to be 'stamped'. Indians, thankfully, are always helpful in pointing where you need to go. Around the corner was a small desk with a few shabby looking men who took my challan and whacked it with a large dirty stamp. Great! Now, back to the bank as fast as possible. But where was a rickshaw?

Departing the Treasury, I noticed, across the lawn and between a hedge, on a dusty road, was your typical Indian tea stall where a few unemployed men languidly hang-out with little to do except nonchalantly watch the world pass by. India is full of these 'surplus-to-requirements' characters, who loiter with a perfect sense of entitlement, causing my Western mind to become strangely ashamed of its rat-race determinism. It was exactly the kind of place a rickshaw was destined to putter by for no explicable reason. And sure enough, after a small wait, along came a ricky, and we were off through the tumultuous, noisy traffic again.

Returning to the State Bank of India, I located the same man I'd spoken to earlier. As I was about to hand him my stamped challan, other customers informed me there was a ticket-system queue. That was the reason for the long line of waiting customers – they all had queuing tickets. To my elation, the official behind the counter waved the others away and took my challan. It was a case of foreigner privilege, which unashamedly I was thankful to accept! Payment had to be in cash, which was considerable, although with solid expectation of refund via insurance. I exited the building, considerably more relaxed.

I anticipated that multiple copies of the paid challan would be required by the police, so I asked a rickshaw driver where a photocopier could be found. He duly drove to a shopping area nearby, and dropped me off at a Xerox shop. Except it was closed. They directed me a few shops down. "Yes" they said, "we have Xerox machine but the power is off in this whole area". They suggested to go down the road and around the corner. Finally, I found a small tin-pot photocopying shop where the power was still on, and had my challans copied!

Paid challan copies in hand, I returned by rickshaw to the Commissioner of Police building to see the passport extension officers. By now, I knew the way and the place well, so was able to direct the driver when he became lost. Again, the passport officers were pleasant, and took my documents, except the multiple copies – "Not necessary". It was fine, they said: wait for a call from the local police to physically verify my residence. Catching another ricky on the big road outside, I made it back to Singarathope, and Julie in GVN. What a relief. And there she was lying in bed as spaced-out as ever, yet always pleased to see me. She ask me to get her to the toilet! "No", I said, as always, "you have to do it in your diaper", of which she never takes any notice. Her constipation problems persist, and are a continual annoyance for her. This needs investigation by the doctors.

For myself, I am feeling slightly better. Despite the demands currently being negotiated, the emotional exhaustion of some days ago has passed. Thank God for that. There is a lot to resolve and I am reassured to feel able to operate sufficiently. The healing support of my friends and the multivitamins, along with having more rest, fixing my computer and clearing many stressful hurdles, have helped put me 'back in the saddle' albeit unsteady. I'm certainly not my normal self, by a long way, yet feel equal to the tasks. I'm reminded of once in my youth, when riding a motorbike while inebriated – all was fine so long as there were no corners!

Wednesday, February 19 (day 24)

Morning

Julie continues to improve, but slowly. She is off the sedating medication and more alert, yet still plagued by bowel cramps. As she had intestinal pains last night, it was investigated by ultra-sound. "Nothing wrong" was the report. Everything is looking and working well, except obviously, she is still having bowel cramps. The doctors explain this as a supine consequence. I am trying to address it with the right food but she lacks interest in eating. Still, she did make a reasonable fist of the chicken pasta last night, and some fish.

Her pelvic fracture is a hairline or stress fracture of the hip cup. If it aggravates, that will mean a serious operation. I researched this on the internet; the standard answer is complete rest for 4 to 8 weeks. There is nothing a physio can do to help heal the bones – they heal in their own time. A physio can help keep the hip mechanism flexible by passive movements, but Julie is active with her legs so that's not a big issue, as long as she isn't sedated.

The current plan is to allow for another three weeks of non-weight-bearing regime. Next, two weeks of gradual weight-bearing up to walking, by which time the wrist will also be ready for light use. This time-frame depends on the x-ray results. If she shows quicker bone healing we may be able to reduce that time-frame by a week, but Dr. Senthil is taking the safe, conventional approach. I have found calcium enriched biscuits but there are precious little calcium supplements to be found. Milk remains the main source.

I asked the insurance case manager about ship repatriation: they only allow that in cases of severe lung problems that obviate flying. Otherwise, it is a big risk if one is way out to sea and requires a helicopter to evacuate.

Christa Luvalla, one of the staff from the Australian Consulate at Chennai, flew in to Trichy today. She sat with me in the lobby along with Mani, the Managing Director of the Hotel Royal Sathyam, and discussed the issues surrounding our case. Christa also visited Julie in the hospital. I am impressed with the efforts the Consulate staff have made to help us.

Afternoon

There is no reason Julie shouldn't be feeling brighter and more alert. Last night the psychiatrist asked her if she was feeling depressed, and she replied that, yes, she was depressed about the whole thing. What she forgot was that the word 'depressed' is a trigger-word for these specialists, which equates to pills. I discovered today that she is still on a low dose of anti-depressant, yet I don't think that is what is causing her lack of energy. She has no appetite, so they will provide a tonic. Appears a good measure.

I am at a loss to understand why she remains so lacking in responsiveness. She can talk and engage more than a few days ago, but there is no physical reason she shouldn't be sitting up reading and using her laptop. It was only much later that I came to understand the cause.

Evening

I have changed my mind about remaining here until Julie is fit to fly in the normal way. While there was gradual progress, I had confidence she could settle in comfortably at ABC Hospital. But yesterday and today, she has eaten and drunk less. The constipation is consuming her energy, and due to the lack of food over the last three weeks, a regression is concerning. I have asked the insurance company to seriously consider an air ambulance. I know they are investigating this option but until today, I had not felt it necessary. We cannot assume she is going to get stronger in an Indian hospital: at this point, if she's not getting stronger, she is getting weaker. I have no idea how they can transport her lying down, but that is their area and I'm sure they have the expertise. I am very worried I will lose Julie if we don't get her out of India as fast as possible!

Thursday, February 20 (day 25)

Morning

The medics induced a bowel movement yesterday evening, and with considerable pain it worked before she went to sleep. Unfortunately, the colic cramps have not ceased. I gave her paracetamol last night a few times so she could sleep but this morning she was still cramping. I've told the nurse to request a doctor prescribe painkillers to relieve her condition. A few days ago one of the doctors directed the nurses to administer Buscopan if there is pain, but that was a different nursing shift: the current shift know nothing about it. I don't know what Buscopan is, either.

While she has these pains, she's in no mood to eat, or even drink. Dealing with constipation is something I doubt a change of Indian hospital can fix, which is one reason to request a quicker return. A decision on this, by the insurance underwriters, is being made right now. I hope to hear soon.

Meanwhile, I have picked up an upper-respiratory infection. It started with a cough and progressed to a runny nose, and now a hoarse voice. It doesn't appear to be serious but I began a course of antibiotics to speed-up recovery before Julie catches it. The problem is that I sleep directly beneath the AC fan. Julie is in a better position across the room but I have to layer on clothes and covers to avoid a chill. Alas, that measure was not initiated soon enough. It is winter here, and cold viruses are common.

Dealing with the cultural and language problems in a hospital for Julie's needs is enervating. Occasionally, I lose my temper.

Late Morning

They gave her Buscopan, the antispasmodic, which had previously been prescribed. This looks sensible, though my persuasion was still required. Let's hope she will feel better through the day, and she may need to sleep more following the difficult night. It will be interesting to see how she is in an hour's time. She hasn't eaten again today, so far. If only she could have some respite from these complications which divert her from feeling normal. Otherwise, she appears clear. Even if we do manage a return flight, it is unlikely to happen for a few days so she still needs to begin eating, and reading.

The doctors say her wrist is healing, but due to the other problems she is likely to bash it against the bed rails, so the plaster will remain on a little longer. They informed me this morning that the side wound from the pleura drain tube is healing. Things appear to be improving, yet her ability to feel normal is an elusive step that never arrives. I have been telling myself she will be 'right' in a day or two, but that has gone on for too long, which is most confusing and worrying. Even losing weight will be something she will be thrilled about once she recovers, but now it represents depletion of the energy essential for bone repair.

Afternoon

I am becoming more concerned and frustrated. The insurance medical team nurse phoned me, and while I stood around in the market street, we talked through the issues Julie is facing. They consider an air ambulance is only a last resort. We agreed that resolving her bowel cramping must come *before* any travel options.

This afternoon the Buscopan did not work. It may have reduced the frequency of cramping slightly but it was ineffectual. She doesn't want to take in food or liquid while she is suffering from these spasms. It is a purely instinctive reaction: if there are problems at the outlet then anything going in will exacerbate it! In between cramps, I convinced her to have a small cup of protein-vitamin mix in milk. After that, she wouldn't even have water.

I had to do something, so I went to the nurses' station and stood there telling them to call a doctor. Finally, the nurses came in as Julie was having a cramp, and it was clear to see the pain she was in. Before long, they had painkillers from the duty doctor and administered another Buscopan injection.

Evening

I have returned to the hospital again, about an hour later, and she is sleeping. So that medication has worked. Will I convince her to eat tonight?

The colic spasms have continued for about three days, or longer in a milder condition. If this could be resolved, I'm sure she would eat and function better, so that is the priority. The insurance nurse assured me that in these conditions, Julie doesn't require much food. But that's different from eating nothing for three days after having eaten so little for the past three weeks. Anyway, the plan is to resolve this bowel problem first. Then we'll decide on the next part. If she is able to eat dinner tonight, I will be happier, and if not, I'm not sure what I can do, except make enough fuss to get *something* happening. The insurance nurse, who is a man, which is handy when dealing with men here in India, will call the doctors at the hospital to push for action on this colic issue.

Searching for something Julie would like to eat, only to find she won't eat or drink anything is exhausting. All the same, there's little else to do. As for thumping people, it's the nurses I'd like to thump, but they are so tiny one wouldn't even consider it! What I would prefer to do is pull their heads together and give them a good rattle. They are sweet but sweetness doesn't cut in these situations. The doctors don't need thumping: they just need finding.

In spite of the agony Julie goes through she can be exceptionally funny and lovable at times, especially when she is completely spaced-out. One time when she was in pain from wanting to go to the toilet, I mentioned something about Australia. She replied that she didn't care about 'scratter'. Next she began moaning, "Oh, I just want to do a scratter. Please, let me do a scratter!"

Friday, February 21 (day 26)

I nearly lost my temper. Almost turned violent to get action happening. I was sorely tempted to throw the nurses' station over the balcony! Julie was in agony for two and a half hours, and I could not get anyone to give her pain relief. Two doctors came in, assured us she would get painkillers plus a lot of other stuff. The 'other stuff' kept coming but not the pain medication, while Julie was writhing on the bed saying, "It's unbearable". All I could do was sit there for hours while she was in severe pain. I felt so angry, helpless and confused. I am aware that hospital patients often complain, and pain treatments come with complications, nonetheless, to sit and watch her writhing in pain hour after hour is distressing.

I have no idea what the delay was about. I kept going to the nurses, and they were happily chatting away to each other. They told me some crap which sounded totally irrelevant. Finally, the English speaking nurse said something about the pain medication not being available, and that they would get something else. I was beside myself by then and yelled, "Christ, it's been two hours! Hurry up and get whatever!" I wasn't pleasant about it and noticed people looking at me, but they did get 'whatever'. I hope it works.

Meanwhile, earlier, there had been a discussion with one of the doctors that despite the ultra-sound showing normal, Julie had been in pain throughout the day. There must be something wrong! They decided to do a CT scan, which later showed everything normal. We have a problem: her scans are showing all systems normal but she is in agony from colic. I am at a loss to know what to do. She doesn't want to eat or drink so finally they put her on a hydrating IV drip. It is not an easy situation. There must be a problem causing these cramps all day and night but no one knows!

I don't think this is a case of incompetence by the hospital (except for the delayed pain killers! – and I'll be telling the head man about that), it's one of those situations without an easy answer. Now I suppose, she will awaken in the middle of the night with returned pain, and I will have to wake up these stupid nurses to get them to do their job. It's been a very long day, and I am once again exhausted.

Saturday, February 22 (day 27)

Morning

It was a rough night. The registrar, Vivek, who is promising, was there when I returned for sleeping. He had administered Butein, a gastric anti-inflammatory, to calm things down. Then, they put her on a continuous drip of Pantodac, a general gastritis treatment, for five hours through the night. Mythili came down from ICU to set it up – the first machine didn't work so she had to get another. She is so calm and competent that I always feel relieved when she is around. This medication worked well through the night except a few times when Julie awoke with pain.

She has required little in the way of pain killers until now – in fact, not any for at least a week or more, because she only had a mild condition. The constipation appears to have ceased but the cramps haven't. The current thinking is that it is an ulcer which has been exacerbated through lack of food and fluid. I will confer with the doctors today but I don't think they have more to offer. At least Julie now accepts that not eating has probably made this disorder worse. Still, she will have little interest in food while she is suffering.

Late Morning

New prognosis: Julie has antibiotic-induced colitis. I Googled the symptoms and this assessment looks accurate, as she had something similar a few months ago despite the different symptoms. At that time, it was painful stomach bloating, while this condition is in her colon. All antibiotics and other medications have been withdrawn. Thankfully, she has certainly improved this morning – the pains are less and the intervals longer.

I'll request that the insurance medical team arrange a specialist consultant to talk with the local hospital physician. I am aware that a specific antibiotic is sometimes prescribed for this condition, but considering the medications she has been on for the last month, terminating them all is wise. We will see how she feels through the day.

Afternoon

A forward step! At last, this diagnosis appears correct, due to sustained improvement today once all medications were ceased. She is now sleeping soundly, having taken in fluids, although still not enough. Nonetheless, if the trend continues we should be back to some semblance of normality in a few days.

The risk with ceasing antibiotics is that a chest infection may persist from the inserted drain tube. This is a question for the insurance medical team, with whom I will consult. I am so happy that she is no longer racked with griping pain. When not in pain, she comprehends my explanations about how her malady is being treated, although she still wants it fixed immediately!

A doctor explained what they believe were the problems. Earlier, she had a compacted faeces lump in the colon, which caused pain as the flow had to get around this lump. That cleared with inducing motions but then she developed colitis, an inflammation and aggravation of the colon. Perhaps … it sounds a reasonable diagnosis but I am so pleased they found the right course of action, which has had immediate results for Julie's sanity.

Evening

I have finally pulled the plug on this evacuation dithering, and written a forceful and informed summary of Julie's condition to the insurance team, stipulating that she must be air-lifted back to Australia as soon as possible. Attention to this had become deflected by Julie's recent ailments but today she has improved. That improvement has demonstrated she is not strong enough to wait out her recovery in India.

Extract from my email to the insurance team:
> Air lift:
> Up until last Sunday I had confidence she was physically strong enough to relocate to a more comfortable room at ABC hospital, and recuperate there for the time before flying out. I now no longer believe she has the strength to do this. She has been significantly weakened by this last few days of pain and starvation. She appears to be recovering from the colitis, but she is so weak, if another incident occurs to set her back, I don't think she would have the strength to even fly out of India. After seeing her this evening, I am now convinced we must get her back to Australia as soon as possible. This may well be the last opportunity. Her mental status is also being impacted by this latest trauma. I am severely concerned for her survival if any time is lost in repatriating her.

By tomorrow morning I should know if Julie is going to build sufficient strength to undertake the necessary flights. Dr. Senthil informed me earlier this week, that he will x-ray this weekend to ensure the rib fractures have healed sufficiently to cope with aeroplane pressures. If all goes well she should be able to fly by Sunday 23rd or Monday 24th February, but I don't believe we can risk the translocation plans to ABC hospital. She has become too mentally and physically depleted. She asked me today, "when are we flying out?" Even she has realised the situation. Later, she told a nurse she thought I had flown back to Australia, obviously confused by our discussions.

I have consulted again with Dr. Senthil, and he is in agreement with the plan to have Julie ready for flying by Monday. Further delays incur serious risk, but can the insurance team organise everything that soon? Last Sunday she appeared to be growing stronger, and would be able to sit out the time in ABC hospital. This recent colitis bout has changed that dramatically. She still has residual strength but that will be required for the flight. I am seriously worried she will die here in India if I let things drift. She must return to Australia as soon as possible.

Dr Senthil explained that her white blood cell count shows infection, albeit decreasing. They could not discern a location for the infection; likely sources were showing good signs of healing. After developing colitis then ceasing all antibiotics, she has responded well. Although she still gets cramps they are greatly lessened. Meanwhile, if she doesn't begin oral intake of food by tomorrow, they will put her on a nutrient IV bag which she had in ICU.

We have to hope the insurance team organise quickly without further delay or questions, and that Julie rallies in the next two days to be fit for the trip.

Sunday, February 23 (day 28)

Morning

Julie had a better night, only waking about once each hour with abdominal pain but returning to sleep. She wasn't on a pain reduction drip, merely an occasional injection.

As expected, the insurance company are not going to act purely on my assessment. But I have started the process, and they will follow that through. It's certainly beyond me to take Julie out of India on a stretcher, alone, without appropriate medical support. I also sent a separate punchy email to the Australian Consul, and hopefully, they can influence the insurance decision.

To make things more difficult, our visas ran out yesterday, and this morning neither of our phones work. The USB internet dongle works, because in Thanjavur they sold me a new SIM without any 'foreigner' rigmarole, which was an error on their part – a mistake I am exceedingly grateful for! Otherwise, I would be completely cut off from everyone. I will try that approach for the phone SIM at the local Airtel shop later this morning. Maybe they will make the same error, if I ask for a SIM with a smile.

Mid Morning

The Australian Consul in Chennai, Tricia Martino, has been exceedingly helpful since this saga began. Now she has responded to me regarding their actions. They sent a copy of my email to the Consular Emergency Centre (CEC) in Australia, who spoke with Covermore. After all this time, I finally discover exactly who these people are that have been handling Julie's case. I guessed it would not be the insurance company itself but an agent for case management. The CEC said that Covermore are in consideration of our request, but not yet accepting that Julie's condition is sufficiently serious to warrant a medivac to Australia. They are going to reassess the situation within twenty four hours.

I know Covermore had been examining the air ambulance option, as so they should. I also know they see it as a last resort, which is fair enough. By my pushing for this, they should prepare the arrangements without necessarily informing me. Now that I have given a detailed assessment and reasoning to them, what they are waiting for is confirmation from the medics: both their team and the hospital. I must speak with Dr. Senthil about my appraisal and concerns, so we are both talking from the same sheet. His word will carry far more weight than mine.

The insurance contact has told me that they can't pay for Julie to be in ABC hospital, as it is outside their Indian insurance agent's ambit for some reason. I could pay, and hope to be reimbursed back in Australia. So that is another issue, and if we can't get out soon I will need to assess the advantages for Julie's recovery in a better room at another hospital. Perhaps I could look at one of the other hospitals which may have links to the insurance company.

Midday

Julie has begun eating and drinking. This is such an immense relief for me. This morning still pale and exhausted, she consumed four biscuits, a small omelette, drank milk and a large cup of lassi (curd drink, which here they pronounce 'lazzi'). Everyone is happy. Mythili, off ICU night duty, is feeding Julie, and she has a manner that is hard for Julie to refuse. She's better at it than I.

Dr. Senthil and I had a productive conversation about Julie's return to Australia. He agrees that this is the best option for her, and said he will speak cogently to the insurance contact. Meanwhile, if we can't drag the insurance company to a medivac, and we have to stay here, there may be an option of another room which I inspected here in GVN. Through the door of that room, the large neem tree would be visible. Unfortunately, Julie would have to choose between looking at the tree or the TV. There aren't sufficient security features that will allow me to move into the room, but if I'm around the corner in the hotel, that is reasonable. We all agree that repatriation to Australia is the priority, second to Julie's appetite returning. Dr. Senthil's approach to the insurance company will emphasise the insufficient level of rehabilitation services available in India for Julie's recovery.

My primary concerns and arguments are, firstly, that Julie has lost so much strength over the last week she hasn't the reserves to deal with another complication, which could easily happen. Secondly, for her state of mind, to even be on the way back to Australia would give her a huge boost, and in Armidale Hospital she would brighten up quickly and regain strength. I told the insurance case manager they are now on a high risk strategy with Julie's health.

Late Afternoon

Julie continues to improve. She still has occasional griping bowel cramps but noticeably ameliorated. The people at GVN are so nice to us. I mentioned room 28 would be suitable because Julie could look out the door at the big neem tree in the hospital courtyard, and I may have mentioned to Mythili it was a pity the TV faced the other direction. Mythili must have spoken with ward management, and now they are re-wiring the TV, moving it to the same side as the door. They have had workers in there through the afternoon and it will be ready in half-an-hour. Amazing!

Julie said she would like chicken for dinner, so I'll make the dreaded trip across town again tonight to obtain good food from Hotel Sangam. The half-hour rickshaw trip is dangerous – each time there have been frightening near-misses.

Overall, I'm feeling exhausted from everything this week. Even Julie noticed it. If she makes a fast recovery, I will too. Mythili being there, attending to her all day, hand feeding small pieces of watermelon (which Mythili suggested and Julie loves) takes a lot of the burden from me. The Australian Consulate has been helpful with advice on dealing with the insurance people. They have offered to loan me a SIM card, as I have been unsuccessful in obtaining a new one due to our visa extensions not yet approved.

Here in the hotel, electricians are finally fixing the power. The lights are out – spooky, considering what happened before. I'm getting out. Electrical repairs have continued while I have been staying here in the original hotel. Considering it was an electrical fault that caused the fire, I am sensitive to the power outages that happen while they are installing new wiring.

At first, three large generators were deployed, which was only sufficient power for one floor of the hotel to open. Mani, the Managing Director, who has been a constant source of assistance for me in any problem, told me that the Electrical Utility, which owns the transformer outside (the failure of which was the cause of the whole fire drama) refused to repair it unless the hotel paid them a substantial fee. This they finally did, or so I gather – you never do know the real dealings behind the scene in India – and the hotel undertook a major rewiring to ensure no further problems would occur.

Having the lights go out continually, leaving everyone in the dark without a lift, only the stairs, carries traumatic memories for me. Nonetheless, I keep calm, and carry on, although thankful I am sleeping nights at the hospital. Ironically, this hotel is now becoming the safest in the whole area, following the alterations undertaken with expert engineering advice. I would definitely stay here again if I returned to Trichy. I doubt Julie would.

Mani and his family are concerned for Julie's recovery. He takes this whole issue personally. Even his little boy keeps asking him how 'madam' is doing, so Mani often stops me as I pass to enquire of the latest developments. He also comes to our room in the hospital along with the ever-helpful and ever-ready Sathish. Julie hasn't a clue who these people are, and despite me explaining every time, she immediately forgets, and wants to be left alone without these strangers in the room.

Monday, February 24 (day 29)

Morning

More improvement! For dinner last night Julie ate a chicken and rice dish with salad, from Hotel Sangam, and she slept well with only minimal bouts of pain. This morning she was asking about passports and flights, so at least she is thinking beyond her immediate physical problems. Perhaps she might start talking, which she has done rarely since this whole thing began.

There are problems with the new room and the direction she faces. Awaking this morning, I noticed that with Julie's bed facing the door, enabling her to see the Neem tree and the TV, anyone passing by outside gets a perfect view right up her nightie. This is not going to work! I stood there in one of those moments, realising there was no one else to ask. Tired and bedraggled from a broken night's sleep, a solution had to be found immediately. Finally, I saw a compromise. By turning the bed on a 45° angle, she can still turn her head, and I could easily swing the bed back when she was in a modest position with a sheet over her. Unfortunately, Julie is not conscious of modesty or sheets at present, so it has to be monitored.

A little bird whispered in my ear that to secure action from the insurance people, I need to phrase my concerns in the following terminology: 'insufficient level of care' in India. Everyone has their trigger words, so that's fine – it's merely a way of phrasing things and joining up the dots. My biggest worry is that since she has developed antibiotic colitis, which can become a serious disease in itself, she is vulnerable to complications where antibiotics are essential. This includes simple food poisoning, which is always possible in India, especially as her natural immunity will be low. That, along with her depleted state from last week, the untreated trauma and memory issues, all adds up to 'remaining in place' being a serious inadequacy of care level. And there is the question of my own ability to sustain support, especially considering the language and cultural problems we face. I will be talking with the Covermore team soon.

Late Morning

I again emphasised to the Covermore nurse about my request for immediate medivac. Being without a phone for three days – the Consul's SIM will take that long to arrive – communications with them have to be via Skype on the computer. Now it is in their hands. I have no idea if they will act on this or not, but the important thing is that Julie is recovering. She is talking and even asking for food, so appetite has returned and normal personality surfacing. The room change is working well. She can turn on her good side to look out at the Neem tree, and we can swing the bed a little for her to watch TV – not that she has shown interest in that. Also, passers-by don't have a clear view of her diaper! Mythili is often there, feeding and entertaining her, which frees me. Aside from the extreme fragility of the situation, I am happy with her status presently.

Poor Mythili does appear fatigued though. Sitting beside Julie all day is not the most riveting task but she never complains, and is extremely fond of Julie. Mythili tells us that when she is on her ten-day night duty stint, she only has about four hours sleep a day because she lives some distance from Trichy.

The police have been looking for me, as I have overstayed my visa! They should be looking for me to process my extension. Anyway, I believe I'm safe, but not having a valid visa makes obtaining a new phone SIM impossible. It would be funny if they carted me off to jail for visa overstay. That would be the last straw!

Afternoon

Julie 'woke up' again this afternoon. After a rest, I was called back by the nurses as Julie wanted to know if she had to get up because we were leaving. On assuring her that she wasn't going anywhere for some time, she was comforted. She told me she could barely sit, let alone "get up and out". She also said she hasn't had a good rest for many years! Then we talked, as she had the energy to conduct a reasonable conversation.

Her recovery might work against our immediate medivac but I prefer to see her recovering above all else. It could mean we will be sitting out the next month here. Dr. Senthil and I discussed this today: he will push to have us returned as soon as possible, primarily on psychological reasons. Julie is finding the whole Indian scene at the hospital disturbing – the noise, the people bursting in at any time and turning on the lights, cocking the door open and speaking in their customary half-shout, the sudden and repeated intrusions by hoards of, for her, unknown people who stand around and stare, fascinated at a foreigner.

When I came in today she was complaining about the crowd of people filling the room. She told them: "I want all these Hindus to fuck off!" I explained to her that they were the doctors on their morning rounds, but there were about ten nurses also standing gawking. It's the way Indians do things. Australians are accustomed to quietness and fewer people, which I explained to Dr. Senthil. I hope I smoothed things down, and anyway, they like Julie, so she can get away with being eccentric.

Earlier this morning I mentioned to the nurses that we should put up a picture of an Indian God on the cupboard opposite her. They were surprised we would want an Indian God, but at the doctors rounds I saw they had installed a picture of the famous local Devi, Samayapuram Mariamman, whose temple is about twenty kilometres from Trichy. Dr. Senthil thought we would prefer a picture of Jesus but I assured him that Devi would be perfectly fine. Later this afternoon, Julie recounted a dream of a goddess that she had last night. There was more to this dream which she felt was important: she told me she is having a lot of thoughts about her life, and the approach to her work. There was a big issue in this dream about the need to re-evaluate her attitude to India, to take it more seriously, especially Tamil Nadu.

Late Afternoon

I would prefer to see Julie flying out in business class, able to use the plane toilets and only wheel-chairing between places. But the risks in waiting that long are unacceptable, for all the reasons articulated to Covermore. I am dreading that she will catch my cold. In fact, it surprises me that she hasn't. I have been doing everything possible to avoid passing on this virus, as being so constantly close creates a serious risk. It wouldn't kill her but would delay recovery and cause her to feel dreadful. Her lung recovery would be jeopardised, and possibly the ability to fly – this is an example of the risks in delaying medivac.

Covermore may yet surprise me but I suspect medivac is expensive and they will put it off. Pressure from another direction would be a good move but how to accomplish that? A politician would be effective but with the departure of our Federal local member of parliament, Tony Windsor, I don't have contact with his replacement. Julie doesn't have a consistent doctor. In Armidale, she had been shuffled around within the practice since her old doctor had left town, so there is no strong personal connection there either.

A phone call via the hotel: Julie is calling me back to the hospital – no doubt she has confused some situation and is needing my support. This is a common occurrence.

Evening

A new problem has arisen. Julie's mental recovery has reached a threshold where she is acutely aware of her inability to do anything for herself, and that she is lying flat, day after day, with no perceptible improvement. Tired of everything, she just wants to be somewhere else. She is frustrated not even having the strength to sit up, and wants to be back home. Julie has always been annoyed with any form of sickness and incapacity. Full realisation eludes her of the seriousness of the situation, and how everyone has been doing their utmost to make her well and return to Australia. I tell her, but that's not the same as comprehending it herself. I am hoping she will improve sufficiently to use a laptop, which would help her mood, and offer a way to channel her frustrations.

Things are finally shifting. No word on the medivac as yet but there is more talk of us moving to ABC Hospital. I will need to check this with the insurance team, as previously they didn't agree to it. More interestingly, Dr. Senthil believes Julie could be ready for a wheelchair in a week. That means sometime next week she could fly in business class (her latest chest x-ray shows all is well). She would still need the bladder catheter and a diaper. With medical assistance, this might work as a compromise to medivac or delaying for another month.

Night

I spoke with Covermore again. The good news is that they have submitted a recommendation to CHUBB, the insurance underwriters, that remaining for the long term is not in Julie's best interest, which is what I and Dr. Senthil have been advocating. On mentioning the possibility of sitting in a wheelchair in a week, the nurse at Covermore said it would take a lot longer than a week before she could fly business class. To sit in a chair is only the beginning of being able to negotiate a flight. It would take at least two more weeks but realistically, he said, she would need to be able to take some steps, so we are still looking at the full weight-bearing time.

Covermore are not interested in ABC hospital, and if the underwriters agree, Julie should soon be transported to Australia in the prone position. They have Armidale as the preferred hospital destination, and her current GP, Dr. Russell King, as the receiving doctor. She continues to talk throughout the day but remains enervated and unable to self-feed. She finds this distressing, that her vitality levels haven't changed since being in hospital. It also bothers me. Even before this recent colitis week, she has had so little energy, and I can't understand why. It has been improving but at *such* a slow pace. Hopefully tomorrow we will have good news about departing for Australia.

Tuesday, February 25 (day 30)

Morning

BIG NEWS!! An air ambulance (a private jet) will pick us up at 8am tomorrow morning and fly direct to Sydney, refuelling at Singapore, arriving Thursday 27th in Australia. My God, I can hardly believe it. Julie will be so relieved!

Needless to say, there is no chance of taking the day off and climbing to the temple one last time. Instead, I must run around town obtaining exit visas, letters and forms. But it's worth it. It is a pity though, as to climb up to the Rock Fort Temple before leaving would have been so enjoyable. Previously, my ankle was too painful to attempt this although I often entered the shrine at the base of the steps for puja. Now that my ankle has improved, I could climb those steps for some distance. Descending is harder. Phone communications are active again as the Australian Consul's SIM card arrived, on loan until we leave.

Midday

I returned to the Foreigners' Office in the Commissioner of Police building. The Australian Consulate staff have been most helpful, drafting a letter to the Commissioner of Police to assist with the exit permits. There is uncertainty about obtaining these in time, and difficulties around whether the plane would arrive on Thursday instead of the current schedule of Wednesday.

The police are confident, and have asked me to return in the afternoon. The problem with the previous attempt to extend our visas was that there was no date of departure. At that time, the policeman had phoned the Indian Foreign Office, after ten attempts to get through, and they advised to apply for a three month extension, because if medical problems occurred for Julie we could not secure a further extension. But that time-frame openness caused difficulties when granting the extension, and was still not finalised. They had tried to call me on my mobile phone but that number expired when my visa terminated. I have a lot of paperwork still to do...

I received a call via the hotel that Julie wanted to see me. When I arrived, she was under the impression we were flying out today.

I told her, "No dear, it's tomorrow we fly out."

She said, "I suspected as much, nothing ever happens quickly around here."

Then I added, "And if there is any problem with getting the exit permits on time, we will fly the following day."

Whereupon she replied, "Oh well, let's forget the whole thing then!"

Late Afternoon

Returning to the Commissioner of Police office, they had our exit permits, signed and ready. Thank God (or *Bhagavan*)! They informed me that I had not completed the paperwork which had to be uploaded to the Website, like the police report of the accident. Where was I supposed to find that? Weren't they the police? And anyway, I had never seen the report, only vaguely heard there had been one completed following the fire.

The officers here were pleasant and helpful. I was grateful they had completed the extra legwork to finalise our exit permits, and carefully placed them in a safe spot for tomorrow.

Covermore sent me the final schedule:

> Pick up Julie and me at GVN hospital 10:30am, Wednesday, 26th.
> Depart Trichy 11:30am
> via Singapore, Port Headland
> Arrive Tamworth 8:30am, Thursday, 27th.
> Ground ambulance to Armidale hospital.

After informing Julie of the good news, I decided against risking the hazardous trip to Hotel Sangam for dinner, to avoid accidents on this last night. Instead, I chose to return to my favourite local restaurant, Vasanta Bhavan on NSB Road, overlooking the temple tank and market streets.

India was not to let me off the hook so lightly. Through this whole six-month trip I have avoided food poisoning, but it was the regular staff's night off. Whoever cooked that curry gave me diarrhoea through the night, and for days afterwards. What a send-off! All the time I have been in Trichy, Vasanta Bhavan had cooked the most delicious food, except for this one night – the last.

To add even more stress, it transpired that GVN hospital had not been paid by our insurance company for Julie's medical treatment. Dr. Senthil explained to me that once we left, they had no leverage to get the money from our insurance. I knew full well what this meant: this was India, and you can't trust anyone to honour their word on financial matters. After making a number of frantic calls to our case manager in Australia, they assured me the payment would be honoured. I told them in no uncertain terms that they needed to activate it immediately, not tomorrow or later, or GVN would not release Julie, as was their right. They responded that the payment would be completed immediately.

Wednesday, February 26 (day 31)

We were all ready. Dr. Senthil came by and told me the insurance payment had come through, so that was another blessing! Everyone was very jovial. Many people came in to say goodbye. Those who do the stretcher tasks – finding the stretcher and transferring Julie from her bed – were standing by, waiting for the final word. There was, though, some confusion about who would do the tasks and which stretcher to use. People kept changing, and stretchers came and went, for reasons I couldn't grasp. One last obstacle was beginning to frustrate me as time was ticking by: we had to wait on airport authorisation. Earlier, I dealt with a similar problem, when the airport required hospital permission before allowing the medivac aeroplane to land. The Singaporean administration woman for the medivac team had phoned me in alarm at this obfuscation, which they had never experienced anywhere else. "It is India", I told her. And she understood.

But now there was a further authorisation which the hospital had to send to the airport, or was it the other way around? I couldn't quite understand. We were waiting on this to complete before they gave the green light for the convoy to head out. I said, "Let's just go – we know it will be all right, and we are already late."

The doctor in charge wouldn't be moved, so we waited for the call from the airport. It finally came. Down through the hospital we went – a great trail of nurses and security men, and Julie covered in new white sheets with 'GVN' appropriately stamped across them. The kind and wise Nurses' Manager came in himself to prepare the bed with these special white sheets. We passed the Vinayaka shrine, where I made a final puja of thanks. The cleaning women, and others whom I couldn't recall from where I'd known them, were saying farewell. It was a ceremonial procession, as if the Queen herself was departing. They are wonderfully friendly. Into the little hospital ambulance they put Julie, along with Mythili and her nice nurse friend, Kothai.

Mani, the hotel General Manager, had arranged to have his driver take me and himself out to the airport, along with Sathish and our luggage. I can only repeat the incredible help and support that Mani, Sathish and Ethi provided for me and Julie throughout this whole saga. I would have been in difficult straits indeed without their continuous and generous assistance. At the airport there was confusion as to the right place to access the plane, but eventually Julie's vehicle was escorted through a gate. I had to enter via the main airport building with all the security and customs hurdles. Mani knew the manager of the airport (he knows everyone), so he was allowed in but alas, here I had to say farewell to Ram, who had also come to farewell us, as he wasn't allowed past the door security into the airport.

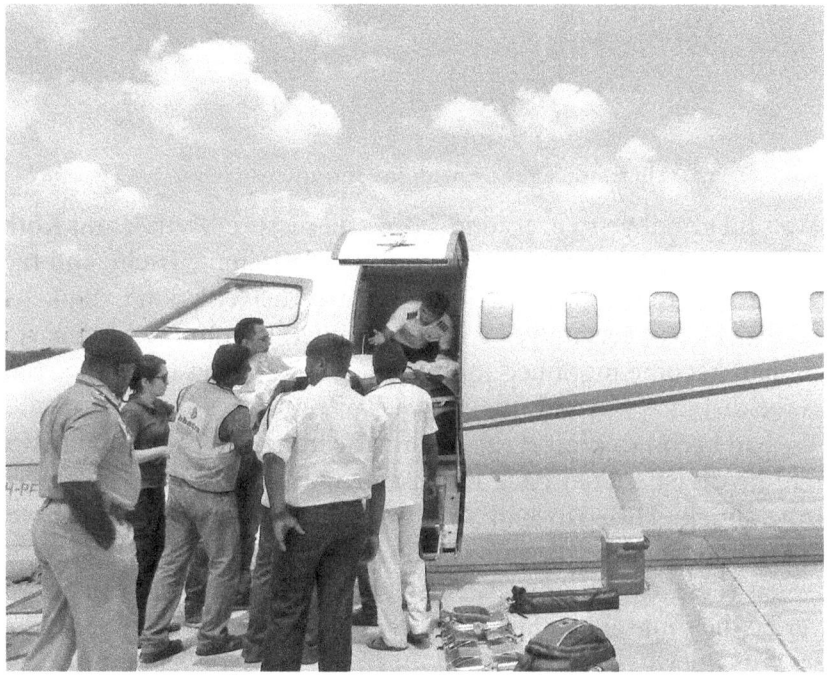

Julie being lifted into the jet ambulance.

Mani's friend, the airport manager, organised a special attendant to speed me through the processes – my precious Exit Permits doing their clearance job – and soon I was on the tarmac at the jet, with Julie about to be transferred inside. It was narrow inside the small jet. I was allotted a seat at the back, while Julie lay on the stretcher, secured on one side of the aisle with the medivac nurse and doctor on the other.

They brought on fried rice for everyone from the airport restaurant. It was a farewell gift, probably organised by Mani. I had taken pills to block me up yet was concerned this food might set my bowels off again. (The pills held.)

Julie inside the jet, with the Singaporean nurse.

We said goodbye to everyone. I can still picture Mythili and Kothai, standing there, waving to us. We took off. Watching Trichy and India receding into the distance, I didn't want to leave. I don't think Julie did either, except certainly, we were extremely grateful to be departing. India had become ingrained in us by now and seeing it rapidly recede into the distance was sad. Would we ever return?

We had become comfortable within the Indian culture, and knew we would be disassociated back in Australia, as always happens: reverse culture-shock. This trip had so absorbed us into the Indian psyche, that I would never be the same again. My spirit would always be torn between these two countries, Australia and India. Julie also, would never be the same again. She had died well and truly this time, and neither of us knew what that would mean. Her old life had passed away for many reasons, and not just the fire accident. Leaving India suddenly and so bizarrely – in a private jet – would leave an unbridgeable wrench in both our hearts. Bloody India! It infects your bones and never lets you rest without a deep longing for its insufferable warmth

Part II

AUSTRALIA

Armidale Hospital

Australian Hospital Experience

After the spontaneous, easy-going kindness and humanity of the Indian hospital system, we were in for a new experience in Australia. What transpired on entry into the Australian health system was an eye-opener for us. Our limited past contact with hospitals had been mainly in Armidale and that memory was reassuring, so we were optimistic at the prospects for Julie's recovery.

Our experience upon landing in Tamworth was, therefore, a disturbing foretaste of our future dealings with the huge bureaucratic hospital system. That included the personal impotence patients can feel when at the mercy of the professional hierarchy, with its entrenched domain-prejudices. And yet, we encountered within this system many excellent people who retained their independent humanity. Throughout our journey in the tunnels of the healthcare edifice, we owe much to the presence and intervention of those priceless individuals.

Thursday, February 28 (day 32)

Morning

We are back in Australia. Arriving at Tamworth airport at 7:30am, there was no sign of the ambulance, to the annoyance of the medivac pilot who had to keep the engines running to maintain the jet's air-conditioning for Julie inside. "This is not India," he complained to the ground staff manager, justifiably implying one expected a higher level of efficiency and coordination in Australia. Three quarters of an hour later the ambulance arrived and refused to take us to Armidale. "We are not a taxi service," they said. They wanted to take us to the emergency ward at Tamworth hospital with a vague idea we would transfer to Armidale later – approximately one and a half hours drive away. After numerous phone calls by myself and others, the ambulance driver sitting next to me was informed in no uncertain terms: they were to drive us to Armidale ... thankfully!

The flight from India had been uneventful; uncomfortable and with little sleep for me, but Julie travelled well once she'd been given a mild sleeping pill. She hadn't required further assistance from the doctor and nurse accompanying us. The toilet at the rear of the cabin had been a contortionist's nightmare for me, and I'd only managed a degree of sleeping comfort by placing my pack between two facing seats and stretching across. We'd flown pretty much nonstop, apart from refuelling. On the first leg of the journey the cabin temperature had been freezing, but after a refuelling stop in Singapore and change of pilot, it warmed up pleasantly. We entered Australia at Port Headland in the middle of the night, landed and took off again in Alice Springs without apparent reason, and finally touched down in Tamworth at dawn.

The ambulance eventually reached Armidale Hospital and Julie was wheeled into the most beautiful single-occupant room, with one whole wall a window looking across the trees of South Hill. The nurses busied themselves with their routines – for me it was a consolation to feel that competent and intelligent staff were taking charge and communication was easy. A young registrar, Katie Gordon, wrote out the full history from the accident onwards, even finding connections I had not considered. She was excellent, and a reassurance for both of us. My friend Dominic arrived, and we went into town for a coffee. For the first time in a month I was relaxed, without concern for what was happening to Julie. I felt in a trance. Everything was a dream – such a sudden transformation from India to hometown Armidale. The light was so different, and the world here was quiet, ordered and empty of people.

Evening

Writing at home, Warrane Station, after a few hours' sleep: I'm feeling half normal, and a glass of wine is helping. The house is looking wonderful. Our house-sitters, Gerard and Jenny, had been perfect in caring for the house, garden and animals. So good, yet so strange, to be home again after what feels like having been years in India, although it was only six months. It's nearly 9pm now, and I have phoned the hospital. Julie is fine. They have conducted the usual scans and changed her catheter, so all is well.

In India, it didn't appear appropriate to deal with an issue I haven't yet raised. Julie has difficulty seeing from her left eye – in fact, she tends to close her eyes often. Katie thought there may be a connection between the small brain bleed and her eye-sight. This means her glasses are not useful and is probably why she hasn't been keen to read or use her laptop. Hopefully, an eye examination will soon be scheduled. The doctor thinks she may have conjunctivitis in her left eye and will treat that over a few days to see if it responds.

I must reiterate: throughout this whole saga, Julie's friends communicating with me on Facebook have been a tremendous help from the very beginning of the saga. Equally, so has been the input from Soma, my online-forum friends. Their comments would extend this account unreasonably were I to include them, but there were constant and multiple communications, with all manner of advice or sympathy for us both, at every turn of events. I am indebted to their willing and affectionate support.

Friday, February 28 (day 33)

Julie rang me from the hospital this morning. She is still feeling strange and isolated, and not fully orientated to being here. Her voice sounded reassuring but she is clumsy at holding the phone, so ringing is not going to be a successful form of communication yet. I will ask the nurse who brings her the phone to check all is well before departing the room. We may need to have phone practice sessions over the next few days. Katie vision-tested Julie's left eye during the day; she could see the fingers of the doctor's hand.

Saturday, March 1 (day 34)

Beautiful flowers have been arriving at Julie's room from her friends. She does appreciate these flowers. They are lined up on the window ledge across one wall of the room – a wonderful array of colour!

In general, I am encouraged by the first day's progress. The staff are astute, and have everything in hand. Julie is still having tummy pains but the probiotics and digestive enzymes should resolve those. She is being prepared gradually for weight-bearing on her feet, so that is encouraging. Mentally, she is responding favourably to being back in Armidale. I'm hoping she will revert to her accustomed self in a few days, although full recovery will take a long time.

Julie was ecstatic about Jerry, one of the wardsmen, who employed a lifter to help her shower and use the toilet. This is the first piece of normality she has experienced for a month! She said he was her favourite man – I came in second. All this time I never could take her to the toilet, and first day back, she gets her dearest wish fulfilled by Jerry. It made me smile.

Sunday, March 2 (day 35)

Every day shows improvement, albeit slight. Today she was less alert than yesterday but fluctuations are to be expected. Bladder training has begun – it's clever how they work on this. The orthopaedic doctor has recommended she begin gentle weight-bearing exercises, so from tomorrow the physios will start their treatments, much to Julie's dread.

The area we are anxious about is the visual deficiency in her left eye. She had a slight infection there which is clearing up with drops, but she has mentioned an inability to make accurate meaning of the information coming in through the eye. That indicates there could be brain damage involved. As poor vision is becoming a source of boredom for her, I will be keen to see what can be done about this tomorrow. Although she is not collating everything mentally, her clarity does appear to me to be improving daily.

Tuesday, March 4 (day 37)

At this point, with Julie back in Australia five days, I remain concerned she is showing so little recovery of energy. Certainly, her speech is better, and she has dramatically improved general orientation to her condition and environment, but she remains flat on her back with eyes closed most of the time. Perhaps I am expecting too much. The ability to use her hands has also increased, and appetite is good.

Her left eye has become an elevated concern. Yesterday, another registrar came in with Dr. Katie Gordon to check her eye. He also did a vision test: Julie could see little with the left eye. They are arranging for an ophthalmologist to examine her eyes: I hope it will be soon.

The only answer we have to the lethargy issue is to push her to use her limbs and her 'engagement with the world', in the expectation that activity will generate energy. Certainly, lying supine doing nothing is not going to help, yet she is too listless to exercise. The doctors appear to be alert and competent, and I have left it to them so far, but by tomorrow there should be explanations as to why her condition is improving so slowly, and what is wrong with her eyes. It will also be time to have an assessment from the physiotherapy team.

Julie's cousin, Joan Anderson, is doing a wonderful job of bed-side attendance through the days. She flew across from West Australia where she and her partner are on a long caravan trip around Australia. As Julie's oldest friend, Joan being here is reassuring for her. Two other good friends, Joan Relke and Frances Gray, have been in, which is comforting for Julie, who only last Sunday said she was feeling isolated. Having close friends supporting her is providing excellent healing benefit. It has also been a huge reprieve for me, in that I feel confident to be away and have some rest. I often wake in the middle of the night thinking I'm still in India, worrying that I'm supposed to be getting something for her.

Many other friends have visited Julie in hospital. Although she is often too tired to engage and then prefers to be left alone, I firmly believe seeing familiar faces lies behind her increased orientation and self-awareness. And the long row of beautiful flowers on the window sill! These things are important, as she has become depressed again with her lack of recovery and inability to see. Even her good right eye isn't working properly. Joan and her friends are doing what they can to bolster her mood with delicious food and drink treats, which I was never able to provide in India and am not especially good at here, either. Their input is priceless.

I have begun bringing in parcels that we had sent back from India during our travels. These are full of treasures we acquired along the way, about which we had completely forgotten! The parcels are a delight to see and unwrap, as they carry the unmistakable smells and signs of India – wrapped up in calico, with the locations they were posted written in large letters on the outside. This makes them totally different from parcels sent from within Australia, quite exotic and alien in the Australian environment: time capsules from another world. Opening these parcels, we are transported back to a such a different place, to another life. A number are still stacked at home, and I've brought in one at a time to unwrap on Julie's hospital bed. Hopefully, the memories and associations, in addition to the beautiful things inside, will brighten her mood. This does help, yet it is necessary to avoid bringing parcels when she is incapable of enjoying the unwrapping ritual.

Wednesday, March 5 (day 38)

We have slipped a few steps backwards. To begin, Julie has a multi-resistant bacteria in her urine, probably from the catheter. It is not currently an infection, it's just 'there'. Now that her catheter has been removed it's hoped the pathogen will disappear. Last night she told the nurses that if they didn't take the catheter out, she would rip it out herself, so they agreed it was time – it has been in too long. More tests are to be conducted today, and she is unable to go downstairs to the physio gym. That was going to begin this morning but was cancelled by a doctor at the last moment. This bug also means she is now in contact isolation at the hospital. Visitors must be careful to wash their hands and use the alcohol gel before and after visiting, while hospital staff have to 'gown up' in plastic aprons and gloves. The physios will visit her for treatment in her room.

The left eye remains a serious condition. While last Friday she could see the doctor's fingers with her left eye, by Monday she could only detect a light. The ophthalmologist, Mark Morgan, is examining her, so we should know more later this evening.

Today, Julie appears more alert, with a good appetite for lunch. We had requested the dietician visit, to organise high protein-energy foods from the kitchen. Julie has lost an enormous amount of weight – over 20 kg since the accident happened. Another friend, Jane Parkes, came in and gave Julie a hand and foot massage which she thoroughly enjoyed. Meanwhile, she continues to be frustrated at the slowness of improvement. I am hoping to persuade the doctor to bring in a counsellor. Also, a visit by the brain injury specialist in Tamworth is being scheduled. That would be worthwhile, although I'm encouraged by her general rate of mental improvement.

Julie has been telling people we were "blown up by Tamil terrorists". This was a dream she had in India a few days before we flew out. Somehow, it stuck in her mind and she came to believe it was the cause of the hotel fire. As a metaphor, it's not a bad one, except that she is well informed of the Tamil's struggle in Sri Lanka. This is a case of crossed wires in the subconscious but when she began telling people as fact that she was blown up by terrorists, I had to explain to her this was not the case – it was a dream she had. She didn't take kindly to being told this: "So I just made that up did I?" she angrily responded, again feeling confused and powerless.

Thursday, March 6 (day 39)

Morning

The ophthalmologist, Mark Morgan, suspects the eye problem is unrelated to her fall. He doesn't know what it is but suspects an inner eye infection, which is serious. He will return on Friday for another assessment, following time for the drops to clear the front part of the eye.

Evening

Mark returned during the day, instead of waiting until tomorrow – he has been speaking with Dr. Phillip Braslins, Julie's primary doctor at the hospital, and the eye infection is now critical. He said Julie needs diagnosis at John Hunter Hospital (JHH) in Newcastle, and depending on the results, treatment there also. For how long, how she'll travel, and what facilities they have for me, I have no idea. We will know more tomorrow.

Today Julie has been in fine metal. She has been wide awake, with improved vision (due to Mark's diagnosis drops), eating and talking – gratifying to see after two days of tiredness. Many friends dropped in while she sat up, wittily engaging with the cross-conversations in the room. This is the best I have seen her since the accident. The environment and visits are producing an important beneficial effect on her general well-being.

She's not happy at the thought of going to Newcastle but saving her eye is a high priority! Unfortunately, leaving Armidale and the wealth of support from her friends, will be a devastating wrench for Julie. This abrupt severance from the life and light of Armidale hospital and friendships, was to become one of the major battles she had to endure over the following weeks in the city. It was to hang in the metaphorical sky like a beacon of hope, always out of reach, yet always desperately yearned for.

Friday, March 7 (day 40)

The story keeps changing. The procedure cannot be performed at JHH Newcastle, so the target has changed to the Prince of Wales Hospital (POWH) in Sydney. This is the only Eye Clinic in NSW able to biopsy the vitreous of the eye. She was going today but as of 7pm she hadn't left and is unlikely to leave tonight; it will probably be tomorrow, Saturday. The difficulty is that she requires a separate room due to the now diagnosed multi-resistant bacteria status. It will be trickier for me to find accommodation near POWH in Sydney than JHH Newcastle, but I've worked out a plan. I anticipate driving down tomorrow – it is at least a seven-hour trip. Julie will be transported by air ambulance. After advice from one of her Facebook friends, I put in a strong request she fly rather than travel by road ambulance, which has been agreed.

Saturday, March 8 (day 41)

Morning

A nurse informed me this morning that Julie may not be transferred for a day or two. She was a bit panicky last night about the move but on receiving a sedative she slept soundly. Also, her 'favourite man' (Jerry, the nurse) is back in to shower and toilet her this morning, so that will brighten her up.

Afternoon

The advice is that transfer should occur on Monday but it's uncertain, due to the POWH room availability problem. Obviously, the sooner she has treatment the better but there's nothing we can do. The medics have classified this as an emergency. Let's hope the delay is not going to have serious consequences. I note, though, that she is using her eye more. Today again, she had her eyes open but is frustrated with the lack of obvious change in her condition. Nonetheless, this is a dramatic change to her general awareness and expression. After a week of good food, and many visitors, she is noticeably improved. Hopefully, this transfer won't set her back, but she has passed a certain threshold mentally. It should be all right.

The main challenge for her is regaining physical control. The difficult and painful physiotherapy sessions are upsetting for her, yet they are beneficial and she is improving. From a physio perspective, two more weeks should show significant development. I was informed in India it would take two weeks for her to walk, and another two weeks to negotiate the demands of a flight itinerary. This timing could extend if further complications were to arise, and I feel there is more going on here than merely recovering from being constrained to bed for so long. We will have to take things as they come.

Evening

Julie remains depressed about her condition, as she can't see any improvement to her fatigue. Certainly, we are anticipating that the physio treatments will be efficacious, though it will be a slow process. The two primary medical conditions are more troubling. She should obtain treatment for her left eye infection but whether it will save her eye is uncertain. Hopefully, it won't kill her!

Possibly, the more serious condition is the urinary tract infection (UTI). They have identified three pathogens in her urine: one is treatable (E. coli), the second is treatable by one antibiotic, and the third is a CRE (Carbapenem-Resistant Enterobacteriaceae) – untreatable by any antibiotic. The danger is that the CRE could enter her blood stream. In which case, mortality is about 50%. In Julie's current state, it is hard to say on which side of that divide she is likely to fall. She is not in a serious medical decline but she has this deep fatigue, which may or may not be connected. Her temperature, at 37C, is within the upper range of normal. She experiences stinging when urinating, so that indicates infection. On Friday the doctors were deciding whether to initiate treatment for the E. coli aspect, or to wait. Evidently, they chose to wait, as she is still not on antibiotics.

The registrar advised me there may be medication to treat the CRE but they are hoping it will just go away, as it often does. I sense she has a better chance of this if she can get moving physically, so I will be wanting to see plenty of physio treatment next week, in whichever hospital.

Julie has a reasonable apprehension that her fatigue isn't going away, so something is not right. Today she has been more lethargic than yesterday. Her energy fluctuates. At least we have found that swallowing slippery elm powder is beneficial for her abdominal pains, and last night she slept without tablets.

Sunday, March 9 (day 42)

Unsure what will transpire tomorrow, I will drive into town packed and ready to depart, and have located a place to stay in Sydney: a caravan park at Miranda. I love staying at caravan parks in our van, which is comfortably set up for this kind of accommodation. I am not expecting Julie to return to Armidale hospital soon. Her primary physician here, (whom she calls Scott Morrison, the name of Australia's harsh immigration minister – saying the only times she sees him he's trying to get rid of her, and she let it be known as he was walking out the door one day) has the view that it would be preferable for her to be where there is access to a larger rehab unit. So, even if her eye condition can be treated in Armidale, it is likely she will remain in Sydney.

Another reason for this difficulty and uncertainty, is that due to the CRE bug, they are not going to be thrilled with her moving back and forth across the state. This could be a good thing, as POWH at least has an advanced infectious disease unit – the best place for treatment. It is not an insignificant condition, so having appropriate resources available is highly advantageous, as our friend Don Webley, a paramedic, observed on Facebook.

I can't be sure what will happen: whether POWH has a room, and if not, what will happen then. Hopefully, there is a place for her and she quickly secures the necessary eye treatment. Also, I am increasingly of the view that her overall recovery is conditional on a good physical rehab program. Not only should she begin standing and using a commode, but she will feel happier once she is able to effectively use her limbs.

This morning she was listless but with an afternoon sleep she brightened up and was able to engage the visitors. Last night she slept soundly – she thought they must have given her a sleeping pill but they hadn't. This was important for me, as it indicated my new scheme, of providing slippery elm, is helping to remove her gut pains during the night. It will be interesting to see if that works again tonight.

Monday, March 10 (day 43)

Morning

I packed the van and prepared everything for leaving the house, Sheena (our 22 year old Siamese cat), and the poultry. Margarete, a good friend of ours, has agreed to come and house-sit. I hope it won't be for too long.

I have a strange story to tell. Firstly, I am extremely apprehensive for Julie's survival. More than any other time since the accident, on researching this multi-resistant organism in her urethra, it presents as the most serious threat to her life since the fall from the hotel window in India. I am not optimistic. Regardless, I retain trust in the whole intent and unfolding of her recovery. But it would be lying to not admit being deeply disturbed by what could happen in Sydney.

Secondly, during our trip overseas, an unwelcome visitor had moved into the garden: a red-bellied black snake. We often have these visitors during summer, and have a technique for convincing them that our garden is not a good place for setting up home: we throw dirt at them whenever we see them (not stones, which can injure them seriously), and we chase them with brooms. You can do this with black snakes but with brown snakes you have to be extremely careful as they are highly volatile. While we were away it wasn't practical to ask our housesitters to tackle snakes in this way, thus an adult black had set up home in the garden by the time I arrived back. Dominic even saw it sleeping on the front step one day. To leave this reptile roaming around while Margarete was housesitting was a problem that had been bothering me, as she would be spending more time in the garden than our previous housesitter.

While we were in Kasar Devi, in the Himalayas, I read a biography of Jim Corbett, the famous tiger hunter. We had even stayed for some days in his old home town, Nainital, so for a while he influenced my thoughts while in that part of India. One curious fact about Jim was revealed by the author: he always killed a snake before a successful hunt for man-eating tigers or leopards, and unsuccessful hunts were invariably preceded by no such snake death. It wasn't that he would go out looking to kill a snake, but that one would cross his path, or not, in the days preparing for a hunt. He became superstitious about this, and always attempted to dispatch a snake that crossed his path prior to an assignment, as an omen of success.

In the days before leaving for Sydney, I recalled this aspect of Jim Corbett. As I don't kill snakes unless I find them impossible to evict from our garden, in my conversations with the spirit of the universe regarding Julie's survival, I put it forth that if presented with this type a ritual opportunity, I would take it as a sign to follow Jim's advice. In anticipation of this, I placed two long handled spades near the back door.

So, you can imagine my surprise when leaving this morning, while carrying my bags out to the van, there, lying fully on the concrete path was the large black snake. I didn't stop to question – the decision had been made last night. I dropped my bags, picked up the spades and dispatched the poor fellow to the netherworld. I have a strong feeling that this was an exchange of lives – the snake's for Julie's. Although obviously I can't confirm that, nonetheless, the feeling struck me most powerfully. The blatant and completely unexpected opportunity to carry out such a ritual killing left me with an overwhelming sense, once again, that unseen forces were protecting Julie: my intent of her complete recovery was assured. I set forth this morning ready for Sydney, with a renewed feeling of optimism – in stark contrast to how I went to bed last night.

Prince of Wales Hospital, Sydney

Brain Injury and Julie's Psychological State

At the time of writing about these experiences, I was unaware as to the extent of Julie's brain injury. It was only much later that the consequences would become clear. We were given little information in the hospital systems of either Australia or India about brain trauma, so it only slowly dawned on us that this was the most serious of her medical conditions. Ultimately, it became the most entrenched issue, as we entered the strange and difficult world of those struggling to comprehend the effects of traumatic brain injury upon physical and psychological behaviour. But one consequence is salient in appreciating many of the events I describe in this story, and that is Julie's emotional/mental temperament.

Post-traumatic amnesia was clearly noticeable, for her short-term memory was almost entirely absent. As time passed, she could remember everything leading up to her fall, except for climbing out the window; otherwise, she could only recall snippets of quite recent events. And those snippets tended to become creatively coloured in detail and meaning.

What was fascinating throughout her hospital time was Julie's psychological evolvement. It has taken me years trying to explain this, because during the experience I was utterly confused, although the practical aspects in being with her were undeniable. Julie was living in a kind of dream state. When lucid, and not suffering from pains or in a sleepy phase, she would engage in her customary way. We could discuss things in intelligent conversation, although I knew that later, she wouldn't remember.

Most intriguing was how she conveyed an incisive, observant and spontaneous response to important things happening around her, while lying for hours on end, almost immovable. Despite being able to move any part of her body when she wished, she had lost overall physical abilities and function. There was a childlike spontaneity in her air, though her insights remained highly mature. It was as if her normal moderating and socially-aware control of thoughts and feelings was absent. It was not missing through incapacity – her frontal lobe had not been affected – but rather through a kind of psychological disdain for pretence and incompetence. Approaching a realisation of no longer needing to play the nicey-nicey game of human interaction, she was now released to 'call a spade a spade', which she did, whatever the situation. It was a spontaneous yet intelligent honesty that caused some people to be wary while others, I suspected, were instinctively drawn to her, attuned to the same realisation of the façade that mostly exists in our interpersonal interactions. Perhaps, for Julie, this behaviour had also to do with being a long time in India.

I found myself delighting in her candid expressions of speech and physicality. These were not always appropriate responses, so I had to chuckle secretly, while outwardly appearing concerned. It often happened that inside, I would be rolling on the floor laughing, while externally acting my 'serious' best to placate or resolve an awkward situation. I relished those moments of dissonance and have retold many of them in this book.

On reflection, I realise this alteration in Julie's temperament, though exacerbated by her trauma, was not solely caused by it: it was a culmination not only of her experiences during this journey in India, but of enormous challenges that had long been unfolding in her life. From all that had happened, in one aspect of her psyche she had passed a threshold of self-acceptance and release from the perennial anxiety for approval: from wanting to appease the eyes of others. Nonetheless, she had yet to moderate that licence in her dealings with those who remained conditioned by these social mores.

Travel in India was critical to this transformation. Indian social values, while emphatic about one's place, still endorse and encourage a claim for self-assertiveness without deference: otherwise, one doesn't survive. It was going to take Julie many years to balance these amplified, contradictory impulses of self-verses-society, and brain trauma is renowned for forcing a deep re-evaluation of this dichotomy. The challenge had manifested in her dreams where she felt enormous pressure to conform to the expectations of 'the nurses and doctors'.

Tuesday, March 11 (day 44)

Morning

Julie was flown out of Armidale at 2pm yesterday, Monday, while I left by road about midday. She was disorientated and tried to ring me but I was out of range on the road at the time. I saw her at about

8:30pm last night. She was in the Emergency Department (ED), in a separate room with a bed that is too small so that her legs hung over the end. An eye biopsy had been taken by the time I arrived. Now, morning, she has been told the prognosis is not good – they intend to operate. "To whip my eye out" says Julie, who is not pleased with the situation. Even one of the young nurses asked me, "Was she like this before the accident?" To which I replied, "Sometimes." Actually, considering the situation, she is holding up well. Yes, she is angry and frightened, disturbed by disorientation, noise and constant lights but she is coping, which is not a small thing considering what she's been through. She has every right to be critical and negative, as developments are not looking good. Once again, I am amazed at Julie's inner strength, despite her free emotionality, or perhaps because of that.

It is very clinical in ED and certainly not patient-supportive, so that Julie is reflecting on Armidale Hospital with fondness. Hopefully, they can transfer her to a ward room today. The noise, the uncomfortable bed and room, are distressing her greatly. The medicos should be dealing with her UTI and intestinal pain with equal swiftness as the eye biopsy.

I had an uneventful trip from Armidale, except my TomTom (SatNav) shot me into the cross-city toll tunnel by accident, so I'll have to go online and pay before I'm sent a large bill. Otherwise, the TomTom was a blessing, although it does take a lot of concentration in the inner city. I certainly drove through places within Sydney I had never seen before.

Afternoon

The infectious disease doctors spoke with me earlier during the day. They still don't know the test results, both for the eye and urine. More scans and tests are needed for blood, stools, liver, heart and brain. They need the full picture, because the possibility exists that the CRE bug can infect these areas. But the two primary areas of focus remain the eye and the urine. No extra antibiotics will be administered before these test results are back, as she doesn't have a temperature yet. Tomorrow we should have a clearer picture. I will wait until the eye specialist has a diagnosis before speaking with him. Otherwise, it's only speculation.

Julie continues to be angry and depressed about how long this is going on. She has had enough. She dislikes being in ED at POWH and is not attracted to hospital food, which bothers her, knowing she has to eat. Also, she quickly becomes satiated.

Evening

Firstly, during the afternoon, Julie was moved to a quieter room, around the corner, down a small corridor in the ED section. It was a cold, unpleasant room but luckily, she didn't have to stay there long. Presently, they took her upstairs to a surgical ward room, rather drab and blank, with greyish painted walls and small window around a corner, not viewable from the bed.

This was a bad evening with Julie. It was one of the darkest days in this whole journey. The possibility of this multi-resistant CRE bug having entered her body and blood, and my knowing the chances of survival were low in such a case (I didn't tell her that), caused serious disquiet during the evening. She was feeling terrible all over. She had a highly irritating skin condition, and generally felt the worst in her body since this whole saga began. She really thought this was the end: she was going to die. I was convinced that was not going to happen but I had to admit the signs were definitely pessimistic.

Julie was highly emotional and accused me of forcing her to come to this dreadful place for her death, instead of our home. "You're a nice guy Michael, but you just don't get it. This sterile room in this horrible city is the worst place I could ever imagine to die. You've made me die in a computer box, instead of taking me home to die in my own house with my garden and cat around me. It's your fault I'm dying here."

There wasn't a lot I could say. It did look like a grisly end was at hand. It was only my conviction that Julie would survive that supported me, because the facts appeared to be pointing to a serious infection.

Julie having only just been moved into this room, and myself newly arrived in Sydney, I'd had no time to do anything such as putting pictures on the wall or making the room homely. I left, hoping she would survive but feeling distressed.

Wednesday, March 12 (day 45)

Morning

I spoke with Julie on the phone this morning, and she was significantly improved, thank God! The conditions of yesterday evening had evaporated - her stomach pains had gone and she reported feeling physically much improved.

But by the time I arrived at the hospital, she was in an aggro-insecurity-boredom-emotional state. I came in late, because, knowing she was feeling better, had gone exploring to find posters for the room. If she was going to die here, Julie wanted something she loved, like the sea, on the opposite wall. I discovered the huge Miranda shopping mall where our own photos could be enlarged, and also purchased calming herbal teas. Due to my late arrival, she had deteriorated into a panicked and distressed mood, believing I was conspiring to kill her for her money! She demanded to ring Tony, her brother, and she warned him I was trying to 'do her in' – to go to the police if she died. Tony was a bit shocked at the whole thing but handled it admirably.

The infectious disease doctor dropped by later to inform us of Julie's status. The CRE bugs are no longer in her urine! There remains an E. coli bug which is easily treatable, and medication for that will begin tomorrow. The other infections have vanished from her urethra though he could not guarantee they were absent from her intestines. When I told him of her physical turnaround overnight, he thought it was possible that the antibiotics prescribed for the eye condition were also benefiting her digestive tract.

He explained the eye biopsy had not revealed anything definitive, so she was being treated with a broad-spectrum antifungal and antibiotic, which could also be effective against gut bacteria. The result, medically, is that she is only staying in POWH until her eye infection is controlled. I don't know if that is happening. Julie tells me that no eye doctors visited her today.

Once the eye infection is satisfactorily dealt with, she will return – but to where? The Rehab people came by to conduct an assessment and write a report. Afterwards, they told me she would obtain better treatment at Tamworth for her brain injury, which they say is still a big factor. The brain scan from yesterday showed no concerns, but bruising and swelling can remain: the brain takes time to heal. This could be affecting her mood, though that's probably as much the trauma of these hospital moves and having not been outside a ward room for two months. They assured me there are superior services at Tamworth to rehabilitate brain trauma patients.

I described to them our dilemma: that what is affecting Julie most is isolation from friends and familiar surroundings. She wants to revert to Armidale, and definitely does not want to be trapped in another blank hospital room in Tamworth. She is suffering from the environment at POWH which is thwarting her trauma recovery. I suspect Julie's feelings on this are accurate, that Armidale's familiarity and friends outweigh the benefits of specialists at Tamworth. Surely, we can find a psychologist and counsellor in Armidale!

Unfortunately, I doubt we convinced the Rehab doctor. She may be reassigned to Tamworth without our consultation. I'll need to act on this tomorrow. POWH is a weird place, where doctors are impossible to find; will they confer with us before they relocate Julie? Will they transport her by road? Anyway, I don't anticipate any movement for some days, possibly not until next week, and we may be detained here considerably longer. I haven't said that to Julie, who is hoping she will be transferred tomorrow.

Trauma

There is confusion around the word trauma, being used to describe both severe physical impact and also psychological impact. Julie has received a physical trauma to her brain but she has also been through an intense psychological trauma. One moment she was in her best condition for decades, then there occurred the terror of the hotel fire, of being trapped in a smoke-filled room, and the whole drama of trying to escape from a third story window on a rope. That was so terrifying she passed out! Next, awaking days later in a weird room, which she believed was an airport transit lounge, with complete loss of memory as to how she came there, to find her body incapacitated and under constant fatigue. She has not seen the outside world, except through a window in hospital at Armidale. Travelling in India for five months, a month in an Indian hospital, transported overnight directly to Armidale Hospital in Australia, then flown to Sydney! Realising she is to lose her eye, and about to die from an incurable infection. Thrust from hospital room to hospital room without clarity about her arrival in this state; in fact, she has been emotionally incapable of even listening to talk of the fire accident, which she believed to have been a terrorist bomb attack. All is condensed to one word: trauma. Where is the acknowledgement, let alone treatment, of the emotional ordeal? Something absolutely critical in the healing process is palpably absent in this medical system!

It is clear to me that not only is Julie holding herself together in the most incredible way, but that she is suffering from an extreme psychological trauma, about which I have been incapable of obtaining advice from the medical professionals. The only information I have seen was in a book Joan Anderson (a psychologist) has loaned me. Thus, I feel no confidence in extending any credibility whatsoever to these professional medicos. As far as I am concerned, they have a long way to go to earn my respect in advising us as to her overall best interest! I am beginning to seethe with frustration at the lack of common sense and basic intelligence within the medical system.

I have been striving to steer Julie through this catacomb of anguish and near-death, hopefully, into the sunlit freedom of the outer world. My only support has been family, Julie's Facebook friends and those on my own forum. Everyone else is a specialised technician, who regard her condition solely from within the narrow myopia of their own discipline. I confess to often feeling completely isolated in the responsibility of navigating Julie through this traumatic saga. People offer snippets of help, but it always falls to me to assess and make the critical decisions that could mean life or death at any fork of the road. I must remain constantly alert to every twist and turn, every technical detail, every emotional and psychic upheaval. Although I have to manage this from my side, she has had to sustain herself through the heart of this turmoil. That she has continued to do so is testament to a deep power she possesses within her being. I am proud of her.

I will consult with the psychologist tomorrow. She interviewed Julie early today – they do have a psychologist on staff, though not in an influential position, which I was to discover is a general rule in hospitals. I want to discuss with her about counselling. Julie needs to talk through a whole history of issues she has experienced over many years. Vicki, one of my online friends, spoke of the need for an advocate within the system, which is exactly what we don't have. At least the doctors are conducting the physical-medical aspect competently. I am Julie's only advocate within the health system; her main complaint is that there are no human beings to be found! The one man she liked, a nurse, John, who is older and wiser than the others, was off today. In fact, we never saw him again.

Afternoon

I organised a cup of camomile tea, which calmed Julie down following an emotional day, so that by around 5pm she was stabilised. We were able to converse with a few friends over the phone, which was healing too. I can source calmative herbs to help with her nerves and emotions, so won't ask the psychiatrist to prescribe anti-depressants yet. Julie was terribly sorry she had gone 'off the rails' in the morning; it disturbed her greatly that she was so vulnerable to these delirium episodes.

This is a good example of how Julie depends on me for her emotional and mental stability. She tells me that as soon as I arrive in the morning she immediately feels better and safer. When I didn't turn up until late morning, she spiralled into a pit of anger, fear and delirium. She understands this – she explained it to me, of how she relies on me to keep her sane, and how my absence caused her to flip out. She is drawing heavily on my energy for her healing, which is fine by me – I have plenty to share with her at present. I arrive about 9am in the morning and stay with her until she drops off to sleep around 8:30pm. The later I leave, the harder it is for me to find somewhere to eat on the way back to the caravan park.

Night

Sometimes she goes to sleep early but I wait until at least 8pm when the nurses change shift, to speak with the night staff. This is important, as events happen through the day which alter their required response at night. Julie almost always rings me during the night in a state of disorientation. Mostly, she only needs to hear my voice, but often I have to contact the nurses' station to bring her medications, which we have previously arranged are available to her. There are times when I ask the nurse to call up the duty doctor, to prescribe something outside the scheduled medications. It is a full time support I am providing as she is particularly fragile and emotionally insecure. She doesn't like Sydney at present, or the kind of impersonal 'city vibe' many of the nurses have: "They're all too young and spiffy-do."

Thursday, March 13 (day 46)

Morning

Julie slept soundly last night, aside from waking at midnight and 5am. She had slipped into sleep at 7pm last evening, which should restore her strength. This morning, when I arrived, she was the best I have seen her yet, and was chatting to the psychiatrist. I expressed a request for a counsellor and our preference of returning to Armidale.

The primary medical issue now defaults to her eye – in fact both eyes as her right eye vision is not so good either. And, as we discovered yesterday, her hearing on the left is also impaired, so will need to be checked by an ear specialist. This explains, we finally realised, why she has difficulty using the phone on her left ear. She is not yet up to conveying the technical aspects of her condition, so deductions must be made by observation.

Julie rang me twice last night, once on her mobile which finally I left there. Though now the recharger's lost – I'll need to search for one in the shopping centre tomorrow. Sounding reasonably coherent, after everything recently, she was concerned at not being able to sleep. She has trouble hearing me on the phone, which makes these late-night conversations frustrating. The medications for her left eye are not working, as she can't see anything out of that eye. She could see a little when tested yesterday, but not seeing clearly doesn't mean the antibiotics are ineffective. The eye damage may be permanent, or take time to recover – whatever recovery is possible. Impaired vision will be serious for her, as reading is a big part of her life. I remain optimistic that she will regain full vision but it will need a miracle – which have not been in short supply during this saga.

I spoke with the infectious disease (ID) doctor and Warren, one of the Eye Clinic registrars. This time they said that the CRE bugs had not left her urine, as of two days ago. This is definitely not what the ID man said yesterday, as we discussed how E. coli can 'cling' on in the urinary tract while the others can't. This makes me concerned about what to believe. I will have to take it all with a grain of salt, and watch Julie for evidence.

Afternoon

After a late breakfast with good appetite, Julie dropped off to sleep, only to be woken by the physios. She fiercely railed against them, that she was too tired to do any 'eckies' (exercises – never heard her use that slang before). Finally she did stand, for the first time in a long while, but she was angry, swearing and crying – generally telling everyone what she thought of them for making her do this. It was amazing she stood, but the physical and emotional ordeal tired her out so much that she has slept for the rest of the day. She is still wiped-out now and a little delirious (the medical staff's term for disorientation).

They moved her about 2:30pm to a new room, two floors up, and much more appealing – bright, with a good window – and the staff more amenable. I suspect this is not a critical surgery ward. The news is that she should improve by tomorrow, when the antibiotic to deal with the E. coli takes effect. Let's hope so, because it's always unsettling to see her so enervated.

Next, I plied Warren, the Eye Clinic doctor, with questions. Her infection is in the 'gel' part of the eye (vitreous), not in the retina which is fine so far. It is clearing but they still think an operation is preferred, which they will decide on tomorrow, and schedule for the weekend or Monday. This operation removes the infected part of the vitreous and replaces it with a gas. The gas lasts about two weeks when the eye refills with a saline fluid. That should retrieve her sight but if the infection doesn't clear, they will need to remove her eye. This is why Warren would recommend the operation as soon as possible. It is a safer option than waiting for the infection to lift. Typically, there are the usual operation dangers, which scare the hell out of you when they read them out! Then there is the possibility of the infection transferring to her right eye. Grim!

Evening

Julie has been wheeled away for another scan – possibly for the heart. She is being scanned for sources of infection. So far, tests are showing normal: chest, liver, brain, intestines, pancreas and so forth. Add to this her normal blood pressure, temperature, blood tests, and the other typical indicators, she is clear of serious infection, except for the eye and E. coli in the urethra. Welcome news.

They still haven't identified the pathology in her left eye but it's certainly not the CRE. Possibly, her UTI is causing fluctuations of emotion and energy, so that should improve tomorrow. On the face of it, there is cause for optimism except for this question over whether the CRE is 'colonised' in the urine, and whether I can trust anything I'm told! She hasn't eaten since breakfast and has been listless all day, so I'm in wait-and-see mode now.

As for my own health, I have no reason to think I currently have any problems. I'm eating, sleeping and the bed-sitting is easier when Julie is showing improvement signs (except when she is abusing me and everyone else, but I prefer that to her dying!) However, I have noticed a 'floating' sensation on a few occasions. I've started taking Vitamin B, which has fixed this kind of thing in India. Perhaps it's a cumulative lower-level energy drain. I hope it's not the flu, which has begun in a vengeance in Australia, as we saw on TV last night. Julie was watching TV yesterday, which is a step up for engagement with the world.

Warren checked her right eye this afternoon, and it looks good. There is still a problem with her left ear hearing, which they suspect is related to the fall.

Friday, March 14 (day 47)

Morning

Julie awoke upset and confused, due to the new room. I will speak to the nurse coordinator today about the dangers of further room changes, especially now she is in an agreeable one. She rang me at 4:30am last night in a bad state – terribly distressed, with no idea where she was, or why. She wanted to get out of the place and go back to Armidale. I was able to calm her down over the phone but she had been awake some time before she rang me. When I arrived at 9am, she was still anguished. She wanted me to get her out of the hospital. I had obtained herbal relaxants which included magnesium, and gave her two. Unfortunately, later, on giving her a third (it said take three before sleep) she threw up – probably due to having had no breakfast and being so agitated. Nonetheless, she calmed down after a few hours. Still no one opens the breakfast for her, and being difficult to do that even for me, it is beyond her strength and dexterity.

It appears she will undergo the eye surgery, but I'm not sure when. They believe this remains the safest option.

Julie is lucid about what is happening to her emotionally, and that frightens her even more. She is worried she is losing her mind. A nurse explained to her that this is a good sign: those who are losing their mind don't realise it! The OT who tested her for post traumatic amnesia (PTA), said that kind of reflective quality was a sign of her advanced education. I told her Julie has a doctorate, and that I had been trying to get her records changed from Mrs., because if people called her Dr. Marsh she would benefit greatly in her current condition. The OT said she would make a point of that at her next visit. I also wrote it on the consent form for the operation.

Evening

The usual conga-line of specialists passed through, and by the time I came back from afternoon break about 3:30pm, Julie was calmer, having slept. She told me the physios had been, and she walked across the room – much to everyone's surprise!

She didn't become distressed again until towards 7pm, but it was more a deep feeling of anxiety than an outburst. On giving her another herbal tablet – one at a time I have decided – she calmed down. A nurse gave her a sleeping tablet at 8pm (I had to ask three times) with her evening pills, so hopefully she will sleep satisfactorily tonight.

During the day, I told the psychiatrist and the nursing manager of the ward that she must never be moved again, as it is risking her mental balance. If she becomes CRE free, she might be moved to a shared room: heaven forbid, as this is a respiratory ward, where people cough all night long. I doubt they will do that though. Even if she shows no serious bugs in her urine, it can't be certain she's fully clear, thus the risk remains. That's one advantage of being a pariah!

Vicki's beautiful orange and red flowers arrived in the afternoon, much to Julie's delight! She spoke with her brother Tony, and cousin Joan. Unfortunately for them, they get enlisted for phone 'contact duty' when Julie is distraught, as this connection provides a reference point for her. But it is hard on Tony and Joan. Julie often asks me to ring them back later in the day to apologise, and to tell them she is feeling better.

The ear registrar came. A brain CT scan had been performed last night to indicate how the skull fractures may be affecting her hearing. The registrar explained that there was fluid behind the ear drum but that her hearing is fine, and once the fluid drains, full hearing should return. They will not drain it now due to the risk of introducing infection to the brain, so we will see a specialist in six weeks to check if it still needs draining.

The operation on her eye is scheduled for tomorrow ... or Sunday. It is called a vitrectomy and the head ENT surgeon, Dr John Downie, performs about thirty of these a week. There are risks, but the risk of not doing it is far greater. Also, they will be in a better position afterwards to diagnose the infection, and thus to prescribe the specific medication. Following the operation she will remain in POWH to monitor healing. How long? They would prefer two weeks but we are hoping one week will suffice – this probably depends on what infection is identified, and how soon Julie recovers.

There has been no report on the CRE bugs in her urine. Presumably, there is time to wait and do a urine test later. Urine tests are not easy, and Julie doesn't know when a piss is coming on. As the physios get her moving, she should regain her bladder control naturally. Meanwhile, a temporary catheter can be used to obtain a urine sample. She is eating on and off but the upper stomach pains she experienced last Tuesday have re-emerged, though not as severely. As there is a fridge in this new room, I have brought along the probiotics and digestive enzymes to take with slippery elm.

We now have nice big photos of our garden, the creek, and Langkawi beach on the wall. I am struggling to find alternative food for her, as hospital fare is bland – even a pig like me is beginning to realise that!

Saturday, March 15 (day 48)

Night

Julie was wheeled away to eye surgery at 4pm. I sat around reading the Mahabharata – being the longest book in the world, it was a good time to start – and eating her dinner, until she returned at 8pm. The nurse from the recovery ward, who brought her back in, said there were no dramas from the operation. Nothing for me to do as she was sound asleep, so I left for 'home'.

An hour later, Julie rang me. She had a very painful eye, which must have awoken her. The nurse explained she had contacted the surgeons who prescribed pain killers and sleeping tablets. They won't tamper with anything until tomorrow and pain in the eye is to be expected after an operation like this. As she was dropping off to sleep she told me, "I want to stick with you." She had had a dream where people were taking her away. I said, "That's fine, I'm sticking with you too. I'm watching everything and will see you in the morning". She felt reassured.

Hopefully, the operation was indeed 'normal' and they can identify the infection. The nurse will keep watch on her through the night.

Quote from the Mahabharata: "Fate has tricked me," realised Arjuna, "for a deeper purpose."

Sunday, March 16 (day 49)

Julie was feeling better this morning. She was enlivened, she said, because finally the operation was out of the way. She was so happy, and dictated her first message, via me, to her friends on Facebook:

"It's a big step forward today. I've had my eye operation, and feel immensely positive from having achieved something finally. Hello dear friends, thank you for your support and comments."

Monday, March 17 (day 50)

Morning

Dr. John Downie and Dr. Warren Apel came in this morning to check how Julie's eye was progressing. Unfortunately, it has not recovered as well as they anticipated. John looked at me and shrugged, saying, "You win some, and some you don't." This is disappointing but still too early to know for certain – her vision could yet improve over the next week.

The operation itself appears to be fine, and from their point of view, Julie can return to Armidale from about Thursday, but her sight has not returned and they don't know why. It could be infection on the retina, or due to impact issues behind the eye. The optical nerve looks good. They haven't identified the infection yet, and may never, but the anti-fungal-bacterial treatment appears to be working slowly. She will be on that for a month, and her vision could improve. As the doctors were leaving, Julie said, in her typical pragmatic style, "Well, that didn't work."

She is feeling better but tires quickly, which is to be expected. Today, with the assistance of the physios, she walked out of the room and down the corridor, so mobility is progressing. Our return to Armidale now depends on the infectious disease situation, but delaying will allow her to fly. Flying too soon post-operation could affect the pressure in her eye. The reason for replacing the vitreous with a gas is to maintain pressure against the retina so it doesn't become detached. Once the body replaces this with its own fluid the pressure will stabilise, and she can safely travel by plane.

Afternoon

What further infections are there? A skin rash that is causing itching around her upper body, especially on her face, is worrying. This may or may not be related to the UTI. Now that she is on antibiotics we are likely to run into digestive problems again.

Her fatigue has returned. Yesterday was onerous, so this tiredness appears as a natural fluctuation. There remains occasional pain when urinating, so current treatment has not resolved the UTI. The obvious fear is that it is caused by one of the serious pathogens, which they haven't treated as yet. At this stage, standing is of primary importance for her, although fatigue ensures she can't complete the exercises set by the physios. She gave them a mouthful of abuse this afternoon when she was awoken for therapy. On her insistence, they rang me while I was napping in the van in the underground carpark; I persuaded them that one session today was probably sufficient – let's see how she is tomorrow. Also, she has not felt hungry, which is another possible infection-related indicator, or is it only natural lethargy? So many questions...

Tuesday, March 18 (day 51)

Evening

I am reading the Facebook comments to Julie now, as long as she is up to it. There was no visit from the ID doctor today, and no new urine test. Julie has been flat the last two days. At least today her skin itches have gone, and no pissing pains, but she is constipated and that is making her feel increasingly uncomfortable. Hopefully that will soon be resolved, if not overnight then tomorrow morning.

She had pleasant visits from friends last Sunday and today, which have brightened her afternoons. The physios maintain their torture, which is good. Tonight, she told me "I am feeling the worst ever." But I don't think any of the problems are serious, except she is fed up with feeling ill. There is no end to it.

The nurse informed me that Julie is being given Fluconazole antifungal. Side effects of this and other antifungals include nausea, stomach upset and pain, headache, rash, itching, fatigue – all of which she has had. It does appear that serious side effects are rare. One of the side effects of antifungals can be liver damage, which cause many of the above symptoms. I have asked the nurse to let the doctors know if Julie is still feeling sick and tired tomorrow morning, in case of liver problems.

Wednesday, March 19 (day 52)

Morning

Last night, the nurse led me on a bum steer with the antifungal: Julie is not on Fluconazole. Very annoying. This morning I asked another nurse to check her chart, and here are the drugs she is on:

Ciprofloxacin, Nitrofurantoin, Voriconazole

I will be researching these later.

Today Julie completed more physio-walking and sitting in a chair for about forty minutes – with loud complaints and feeling unwell. Aside from the nausea, she is improving but nausea tends to make one disgruntled. She was awake with another anxiety attack last night, and again early this morning, which hasn't helped her mood.

The hospital staff are talking about Julie leaving POWH, but to Tamworth instead of Armidale. No matter what we say, they still believe specialists are better for her than friends who can provide the essential psychological healing. I will do what I can but I remain concerned she will not find help for her anxieties in Tamworth. It is impossible to convince these people of the priority of her emotional state. I can only envision continued disorientation in another strange room and hospital, without the reassurance of familiar faces.

Afternoon

Finally, we have more information – I've spoken with Warren and the infectious disease (ID) doctor.

Firstly, the left eye: Julie's vision has improved dramatically in the left eye – she could see a large R on the chart across the room. Also, the pathogen in the eye has been identified and change to a more targeted antifungal has been prescribed, which oddly enough is the same one I was speaking of earlier, Fluconazole (told to me incorrectly at the time). It is a lower impact drug, and the recovery should be faster.

UTI: the doctors are unconcerned with this now. They will undertake tests but it appears to have cleared up.

Move: either Friday or next Monday, hopefully by plane. I have expressed my views about Julie in her current state spending six hours in the back of an ambulance.

Place: we can't go to Armidale hospital, despite it being our preference, because the Rehab boss at Armidale hospital has flatly refused to accept her, for reasons that are not clear. The choices are Tamworth or Ryde. This probably means we are stuck with Tamworth. Heaven forbid we are left with Ryde, which is in Sydney, where none of her friends can visit. At least Tamworth is only one and a half hours drive from Armidale, and Tony lives close-by. Julie already wants me to take her out of hospital and pay people to assist her privately. Obviously, this is out of the question but I've been gentle in explaining that to her.

Feeling it best to prepare her for the Tamworth option, we have been discussing it casually, so it won't come unexpectedly. Unfortunately, I know exactly what will happen to her once she gets there – she will panic again in the middle of the night. It is not going to be stress-free for her, as she becomes so easily disoriented. Physically, she should make quick progress, especially once the infections and drugs clear from her system. A transfer to Armidale will hopefully not be too distant. We have not been impressed by the psychiatric staff coming around with their little inane tests, and can't see what else they can provide at Tamworth. If they can make new spectacle lenses for her right eye, that would be something practical. I must confess, this refusal to accept her at Armidale hospital by the Rehab person has angered me.

Thursday, March 20 (day 53)

Morning

Julie's left eye vision has improved this morning, reading the second line of the eye chart on the wall. She is suffering from constipation, which is proving intractable. The nurses are trying a hot shower but she is very tired.

A receiving doctor in Tamworth is being arranged, and a flight. It could be Friday, or next Monday. Tony should be able to meet her at Tamworth. They do have skills for her condition in Tamworth, so hopefully that will assist her adjusting to the location change.

Julie rang me during the night a few times, as usual. She remains disorientated. She thought she was in a French restaurant. "It has turned all French", she said. One of the male nurses is French, and he had been on duty during the night shift. But Julie can be funny in these disorientations. One of the funniest events happened during her last phone call about 4am. This is both humorous for me listening, and poignant. She tends to mix up dreams with waking reality while she is in this state of fear and confusion.

In the phone call, she told me she was trapped in a French restaurant with a lot of French people telling her what to do. She said they wanted her to "kill this duck". Then she went on to describe other problems she was having. She was very upset but as we talked, I was able to reassure her that everything was fine and she was in good care. That she was not in a French restaurant – they were nurses, and she was in hospital in Sydney, Australia. Slowly, she comprehended what I was saying which appeared to return her sense of place and stability. Her voice calmed down. I could see she was beginning to drift off to sleep again, much to my relief. Then suddenly she perked up and said, "But what am I going to do about the duck?"

Afternoon

Tamworth won't take us. They don't have a separate room with bathroom – their Rehab rooms are shared bathrooms. Because of Julie's multi-resistant bacterial history she has to be placed in a single room with private bathroom. The next option is Ryde but we don't know anything about that yet. Due to the risk factor, for a long time she will be classified as potentially carrying this multi-resistant pathogen even though they assess it has left her body.

My view is that she should remain here another week, and because they need to relocate her from a critical ward as soon as possible, there is an incentive to reclassify her Rehab status to a level that will satisfy Armidale. She has been scoring one short of full marks on her daily Post Traumatic Amnesia (PTA) test almost every day, so it can't be that serious. Anyway, we'll see what happens.

She is becoming distressed by this rejection from hospitals. She has asked me to write her second communication to Facebook, in this case to my sister:

"Marilyn, I can't tell you how fortunate I am to have Michael's support through this. I'm becoming very tired, and I don't know how long I can do this for."

Evening

It is a tricky situation. On the one hand, the doctors are doing what they believe to be right for Julie, wanting to transfer her to a place that can provide the best treatment for her primary condition. They consider this to be the brain injury. But there is the complication of the CRE bug. From the POWH infectious disease team's perspective, that infestation no longer exists, to the extent that they can't be bothered even doing a urine test. It would involve a catheter, so perhaps they are trying to avoid further exacerbation of the colonisation, were pathogens still lingering. This issue guarantees Julie a private room and attached bathroom but denies her a move to Tamworth Hospital.

As for Armidale Hospital, I don't know their reasons for refusing admittance but considering it was their Rehab doctor, I can only assume that the POWH Rehab team's assessment demands too high a level of care for Armidale. Yet, I don't know this for sure. So while the doctors and administrators squabble among themselves, this is known to Julie, who is becoming increasingly distraught. Were they to say she could go to Armidale tomorrow, her anxieties would dissolve immediately. This uncertainty is adding to her feelings of isolation, powerlessness and abandonment, along with being trapped in weird places and paranoia, which she didn't have in Armidale Hospital.

Thus, as we await decisions that are out of our control, Julie is having to bear the consequences of a condition none of the doctors seem to take seriously: her intensifying anxiety. It is left to us to manage these phases of emotional distress.

We have to chart a course through very troubling waters, to the best of our ability, while the good doctors, doing their best, continue to aggravate her unstable mental state. She is aware of the situation, and increasingly distressed that she may not be able to see it through.

Immediately though, it comes down to how soundly she sleeps tonight, and whether her constipation will resolve. Luckily, we addressed both these issues with the young night-duty registrar, the first doctor with whom Julie felt a connection, and who prescribed stress medication for tonight. She is also one of the initial graduates from UNE's Medical Program. As I am connected with the Joint Medical Program of Newcastle and New England universities, as a software development contractor, I feel a sense of satisfaction that we came across one of their graduates who has proved so helpful in this difficult situation. Good job JMP, to produce such an empathetic medic – I must tell the Year Managers.

Friday, March 21 (day 54)

Morning

Julie walked all the way up and down the corridor without the support contraption, and only the assistance of two physios beside her for 'just-in-case'. Previously, she sat in the dreaded chair, grumbling, but soon brightened up when our friends Stuart and Nancy walked in. She remained in the chair, unconcerned, during their entire visit, chatting amicably with a cup of tea in hand – happy to see them both.

The Rehab team visited – a psychiatrist, accompanied by her student offsider, to whom we explained Julie's problems of anxiety, and her entreaty to return to Armidale Hospital. The psychiatrist said the sedative prescribed last night dampened her energy levels next day, so tonight she will be given Quetiapine. She acknowledged our point about the Armidale situation.

Previously, we had a visit from the Occupational Therapist (OT), who was doing the daily PTA test on Julie. This test is the critical one for escaping their clutches. It measures her capacity to lay down and retrieve short term memories. She hates the test because it's full of inane questions which she lacks motivation in answering. But she knows their significance now, which only causes further annoyance and stress – this is about lack of control.

Julie's opinions are not taken seriously because she is classified as insufficiently mentally competent to make comprehensive and rational assessments. To prove her mental capacity and exit this 'hell-hole', she must succeed in remembering silly little things from day to day – like a knife, or scissors, in addition to the day and the name of the hospital. She says to them, "Why don't you ask me the name of Chief Minister of Tamil Nadu?" Frankly, I doubt my own capacity to pass these memory tests. To be 'out of PTA' she has to score twelve for three days running. Yesterday she scored ten, and today twelve.

Afternoon

Victoria, one of the main Rehab staff responsible for Julie, came in to talk with us, although she may not have been ready for what we told her. The point we were making is that with a score of ten then twelve, she is obviously not in the serious PTA category, and has achieved this in POWH (she scored very low in Armidale) without treatment and in spite of high anxiety. So why are they determined to send her to the dedicated brain injury hospital? This is probably Ryde Rehab now, although with only sixteen beds, it is yet to be confirmed that even Ryde has availability.

Meanwhile, Julie gave a passionate demonstration of the anxiety and depression she is suffering at being denied return to Armidale. I held to the rational argument, while trying to calm Julie. She has become increasingly distraught at being trapped in a powerless situation. We explained that the expert technical support these hospitals can offer is well acknowledged by us, which I had researched on the Web, and our friends at Warrane Station near Armidale where we live, have first-hand knowledge of Ryde's quality. But Julie's current nervous-emotional state was primary and serious. All specialists can do for her, as far as we have been informed, is to prescribe medications as she is receiving now.

Victoria did acknowledge that the natural love and support of home and friends was a superior treatment. I sense she left with at least an attitude that she will do what she can for Julie's wishes, considering how close she is to being clear of PTA, and her physio requirements being standard service in all these hospitals. We had pushed Victoria hard, but she was not likely to allow our arguments and emotions to supersede her specialised assessments: which is perfectly understandable.

Evening

Julie ate well tonight, despite being seven days without a crap. I gather it's 'C' day tomorrow: if nothing comes through naturally, they will administer a purge which is given prior to a colonoscopy. There are bowel specialists here at POWH who are advising on Julie's case. Her white cell count is up – infection exists but not of concern. Generally this afternoon, she was feeling better, perhaps because she had earlier given vent to her fears and feelings.

As for infections, one of the infectious disease team doctors came in to talk with us about India. She loved a trip she had taken to India and wants to return there. Julie enjoys talking about India, so that was nice. Meanwhile, the doctor told us about the multi-resistant organism. Julie had been diagnosed with NDM in her urine the first night. That stands for New Delhi metallo-beta-lactamase, about which we are informed from newspaper reports, detailing the Indian government's reaction to the news of this organism being found in New

Delhi's water supply. The government was so upset at what they saw as an attempt by the UK to sabotage the growing medical-tourism industry in India, that they took it out on the two Indian PhD students involved in the research, who lost their funding.

NDM is a gram-negative bacteria, one of the most deadly with which to become infected. Julie did come close to dying with this bacteria in her system: we were right to be seriously concerned. The ID woman said it had now disappeared completely from Julie's urinary tract. Another urine test will be taken today, so that will be interesting. It's funny who turns out to be an Indiaphile. If only research could unearth a new antibiotic, we would feel safer about returning to India!

Saturday, March 22 (day 55)

Morning

We had more delightful visits from friends. Arianwen brought Julie some beautiful calmative herbal tea. These visits are rare here in Sydney, and due to the highly fragile and volatile state of Julie's mind and emotions, any visit, even from familiars we haven't seen in many years, are of considerable benefit. Since being back in Australia she has increasingly appreciated the value of friendships. I won't detail all those who found their way to visit, but I can assure them their presence was greatly appreciated. It is a consuming task to help Julie maintain her sanity here in Sydney.

Julie asked me to dictate her third post to Facebook:

"It's been wonderful seeing Peter, Arianwen and Zander (what a treat). Old friend Ali MacKay, and precious much-loved cousin Stuart, always very dear. Each day it's revealed to me how much fortune I have in the world. I don't know what I'd do without Michael."

She says that about me when she is feeling okay but I also bear the brunt of her emotional anguish! I don't mind. I understand what she is going through, and if she can't relieve her stress onto me it would be unhealthy to bottle it up.

Afternoon

It looks as if Ryde Rehab will be the place. A Rehab doctor will come to examine Julie next week. They think her left-eye vision will continue to improve.

Night

Another painful evening for Julie. The emetic she took at 2pm this afternoon began cramping in waves around 4pm. She was still suffering them at 9pm when I left but by then she'd received painkillers and sleeping medications so she should have a good night's sleep. Not much has come through yet – if she doesn't clear the blockage by tomorrow afternoon these emetics may be given again. Poor Julie, she wants to know what has she done to be so punished. She has suffered a lot in the last two months.

Sunday, March 23 (day 56)

Early Morning

Julie had a bad night. She rang me four times. She is not capable of handling the mobile phone, so she calls the nurse to help. The painful cramps didn't stop. Hopefully, they will decrease in frequency but there is little sign of decreasing in intensity. The last time she rang was 2:20am: she had a dream that she was being used in an experiment in Texas to cross-mate with cows, and she was trying to give birth to a calf. She blamed me for signing her up to the experiment. She told me, "You need to come in here and accept some responsibility for this!"

I rang the nurse's station – for the second time – and they had administered pain killers a half-hour earlier. I asked them to get the doctor to check on her because I didn't know if the painkillers were working, or what the situation was. The nurse was a nice woman but she was Indian, so it was not easy to have a clear conversation. Indian nurses here are good but in an emergency over the phone I was unconvinced of Julie having appropriate attention.

I dressed, packed up the car and drove into the hospital, but the doors were locked. I had never been at a hospital in Australia at 3am, so was not aware that they lock up. There was nothing I could do, as Julie had not rung me again, so I drove back to the caravan park and returned to bed. She hasn't contacted me since, so hopefully, no news is good news. A different treatment will be required if this constipation persists. Oddly, the x-ray revealed that her condition is not serious – not 'compacted' – so why is she having this pain and trouble? In her current mental state, these problems are distressing. I will get to the 'bottom' of it when I return to the hospital. It would be wonderful if it was resolved by then.

Morning

Thank God, the constipation lifted during the night. She still has cramping but it should ease through the day. She is also standing steadier and sitting longer in the chair.

A big revelation for me: I had been mixing up the doctors. I'm not usually so vague about people but there are so many specialists traipsing in and out of Julie's room, from all kinds of disciplines and sections of the hospital, that I struggle to keep up. The man we both recognise is the Eye Clinic registrar, Warren, because of his fabulous red hair. He is more competent than anyone else in most situations. The mix-up I made was between the infectious disease team doctor who occasionally dropped in, and another Eye Clinic registrar, Matt, who is the doctor immediately responsible for Julie while in POWH. I had mistakenly thought Matt was the ID doctor. This is what caused my earlier confusion about her CRE clearance. It was the ID doctor who told me she was clear of the NDM bug a week ago. The following day, it was the Eye Clinic doctors, Warren and Matt, not knowing much about these multi-resistant pathogens, who still classified her as having them in her system. I was relieved to clarify this in my mind, as it had been undermining my confidence in the hospital system.

Afternoon

We were told by (yet another!) Eye Clinic doctor this morning that it won't be until later next week that Julie moves anywhere.

She is feeling better today, although still cramping – the nurses are managing that with Panadol and Buscopan. There is good reason to think she will have a pleasant sleep tonight, and feel better tomorrow.

Night

Although her abdominal spasms continued in varying intensities, Julie had an improved day. With Panadol or other similar pain relievers, she was able to calm down and sleep. Following dinner, of which she ate a little, the pains grew in intensity. At 7:30pm she was given Buscopan, which didn't help, so at 8:30pm they gave her Ibuprofen, a painkiller with anti-inflammatory properties. I left her at 9pm, peaceful and slipping off to sleep. At 9:30pm her usual nightly medications will help her sleep until about 1pm. They are ready with other measures at that point, so she should be okay.

During the night, she later told me, a male nurse came in (the French man, whom I like) concerned at hearing her cries from the corridor. Julie informed me that initially he had told her to "stop crying", whereupon she replied, "You'd cry too if you'd been through what I have." He was considerate after that and gave her a hot pack for her tummy. Hopefully tomorrow these spasms should subside.

I had an insight into Julie's disorientation experiences. Tired of the same noodle shop for lunch and dinner, I sauntered down Randwick's main street looking for an Indian restaurant, or at least something different from pizza, chips and noodles. This was the first time since being back in Australia that I have strolled without being on a mission for Julie. I began to feel reverse culture shock rising up within me. It had always been there but was masked by being so task-oriented, or sitting in a hospital room. The time at Warrane, in the first week back in Australia, was different because our home is so familiar.

I experienced the same background panic Julie speaks of when she wakes at night, that this is not 'my place': being in an alien world that I don't understand and don't trust. While sitting in the Italian restaurant eating pasta, I couldn't shake this experience. It is worse for Julie due to her lack of control and PTA affliction, but I immediately recognised a similar anxiety. Having been embedded in India for so long during this trip we have both shifted our cultural centre of gravity, causing her to feel disorientation more intensely.

Monday March 24 (day 57)

Morning

Julie received her final medications at 10:30pm last night, and mostly slept until 5am when she awoke with painful spasms. She rang me at 5:30am while a doctor was in the room evaluating her condition, and the nurse had administered another painkiller. At least she had a reasonable sleep but this purging is persisting for a long time. Is this the normal, expected consequence, and will it dissipate today?

She rang me again at 8:30am, and I gathered she wanted me on the phone because she was being interviewed by a Rehab doctor. All I could do was listen: I heard her respond to the questions intelligently and clearly. He asked her what day it was, and she said "Monday". Then he asked what was the date? After saying she didn't know, she looked across the room and saw the physio's chart which had Wednesday 19th written on it. She said, "The 19th. Oh, but that's cheating." Then she said, "But that's Wednesday. 19 and 7 is 26, so it's the 24th today." I could hear the collective gasp in the room, through the phone.

Afternoon

It's been a long day in the trenches. Following an interminable succession of doctors, nurses and god-knows-what, Julie was exhausted, especially as her colic pains continued. After a little lunch, she felt an intense pain in her chest. Blood tests were conducted last night when she complained of it then, and x-rays this morning. No one knows what the problem was, except they said her heart was fine.

About 2:30pm in the afternoon, Warren, the dashing young eye doctor with his shock of red hair, and whom we both like, came in when Julie was experiencing these pains. Following a few hands-on tests, he asked the nurses to bring a drink and pill: for reflux. As soon as she drank it, the pain disappeared. Simple as that! After all the fuss and testing that went on, Warren quickly dispatched the problem with a simple reflux medication. No doubt, this young doctor is impressive.

He completed the usual eye examination, proclaiming it was progressing satisfactorily. Then, he told us the latest news about the move. He said, "Ryde can't accept you because they have no ophthalmologist. Tamworth doesn't have a single room with bathroom, so the only place left is Armidale." He glanced at me and added with a grin, "I'm sure you won't have any complaints about that."

I said, "But they won't accept Julie for Rehab." He replied "I have spoken to Rehab at Armidale, and it looks positive but don't get your hopes up yet."

At 4pm, Julie's main Eye Clinic supervising doctor, Matt, came into the room and told me, "Armidale have accepted Julie. We may be able to fly her up later in the week." When I told her, in the midst of one of those stressful PTA tests, she was so relieved she started crying. But we both know there is many a slip yet, so we hang in here and hope it unfolds as best as possible.

Night

Julie had been given the emetic at about 2pm on Saturday afternoon – two and a half days ago. She is still enduring painful colic spasms even tonight, which are being controlled by Panadol and Ibuprofen. To help her through the night the nurses will administer calming and sleeping medication, which worked last night, so here's hoping for tonight. Meanwhile, Movicol laxative is continued to keep everything functional.

She rang me at about 9:30pm with colic pains. I contacted the nurse who said she will administer Julie's evening medications soon. That should be okay but it is surprising she is still having abdominal cramps two and a half days later, though they say it is normal for her case. Poor Julie has had enough pain through this whole ordeal. Hopefully, it subsides tonight and tomorrow so she can move ahead with the rehab and resume eating.

Understandably, she feels this sequence of things going wrong will never end. This has been an exhausting struggle through interminable ordeals to regain her health, which dangles in front like a mirage but always out of reach. It is impressive, the way she keeps weathering pain, and despite her depression, she exhibits a constant sustaining strength. I can see it, even if she can't. Amongst it all, I continue to sense she has a strange protection.

Tuesday, March 25 (day 58)

Morning

It was another difficult night for Julie. When will this ordeal end? She phoned me a few times in distress. Also, she was becoming disoriented due to troubling dreams. I rang the nurses twice. They must be getting tired of me ringing them about their job. At least, I hope they are. Julie has been able to phone me herself, and answer my calls, so that is an improvement.

One of the dreams, of which there have been recurring variations, is the need to please the nurses by doing successful poos. This is understandable from the distress she has been through relating to her bowel processes. She had a dream last night of being in an underground room, having to circumambulate a central pillar. Somehow, in the dream, this equated with such a good evacuation, she felt tremendously alleviated that the nurses will be pleased with her. In conjunction with this theme, there is the larger concern in her dreams of not upsetting the doctors and nurses – of behaving correctly so they will approve. This is connected to the brain injury symptoms of short temper, depression and general annoyance at things around her. It is a pity her condition is so commonly misunderstood by the mainstream medical staff. Once we spoke to the brain injury experts, it was clarified that these behaviours are acknowledged and expected.

It became obvious last night that Buscopan and Ibuprofen are not working. What helps are Panadol and Endone, and it took a painful night to establish this. Why she is continuing to have these spasms is a mystery. I hope they naturally subside, as it is undesirable to constantly resort to painkillers which cause constipation themselves, especially Endone.

I was unimpressed with the ward's system of documentation. The charts were changed last night, and if I hadn't checked on Julie's available medications, they would not have been brought across from her old chart. Also, when I couldn't recall the exact name, the nurse kept reading out old medication suggestions that Julie does not take any more. I assume these had been prescribed at some point but I had never heard of them; it bothered me she could be given inappropriate drugs. I was not left with confidence in their charting method.

Perhaps I was misinterpreting this situation but the apparent lack of clarity bothered me. Yesterday morning a nurse was offering Julie another laxative pill. Surely she does not need more of that, aside from a little Movicol to gently move things along considering all these analgesics. She has diarrhoea now from the emetic treatment. I will ask the doctors to check if anything could be contributing to her colic. Again, I'm having to do a crash course in these afflictions, because I lack confidence it can be safely left in the hands of the hospital system, without centralised coordination.

One of the difficulties is that Julie is being treated by many separate teams, and a different person from each team often visits. It is very confusing. It is even confusing for them, so that yesterday a man called Jeff, from the Rehab team, turned up to talk with Julie and me, to hear our side of things. All he did was listen.

He said they were trying to tie everything together, and were aware we were excluded from discussions. That is certainly true, except for the Eye Clinic doctors, who are her primary responsible team: Matt and Warren are excellent. They have been efficient in helping Julie and keeping me informed but we are excluded from consultation in the Rehab team's determinations. We talk to numerous different people, who come and go, and we don't know how it fits together or who is critical in the decisions.

If this colic pain can subside, I'm sure Julie will be feeling better immediately.

Evening

Colic pains have gone, thank God! But her reflux remains. A scan of her chest was taken today, to rule out possible blood clots in the lungs. Warren thinks there is little doubt this is reflux but they must be sure before she leaves POWH.

Stupid Victoria from Rehab came in at lunch time, and told Julie she would never make a complete recovery. How's that for a good rehab aspiration? Julie said she felt tired the moment 'that woman' came into the room and opened her mouth. I was going to be rude to her but thought better of it.

Victoria was not pleased that we had won on the Armidale move. How is it these people think they can get away with implanting negative expectations in a person struggling to sustain optimism in the face of insurmountable odds? Well, they can't get away with it while I'm here – I continue to reassure Julie with my intent that she will make a complete recovery, and she will!

I also felt, after asking, that Victoria was yet another person who didn't understand what the brain damage units in Ryde and Tamworth actually do. I pushed her to ensure the brain injury doctor from Tamworth would come to Armidale to consult with us and the doctors there. We still want consultation with these specialists. I had the feeling she was not the right person to speak to about this, so I will talk with Matt and Warren – they are the only ones who do anything around here!

But Victoria reified my understanding that as soon as Julie repeatedly answers these inane PTA questions correctly (which she is close to every day now), the brain injury people would no longer be interested in her because she will be out of PTA. That sounds superficial to me, which I told her, but she stuck to her script: 'we know best'.

Wednesday, March 26 (day 59)

Morning

Julie slept well last night, so hopefully that marks a positive change. The doctors are still examining her lungs. Something there needs to be investigated but they don't expect it will interfere with the transfer timeline. She is very tired today. After the two huge previous days, that is only to be expected.

Evening

Julie had reflux pains again during lunch but not at dinner. I have been carefully giving her a measured sequence of helpful things leading up to food: probiotics, slippery elm, yoghurt, and avoiding acid causing foods. If this evening's results can be continued tomorrow, she will be happy. Otherwise, she slept most of the day. The Temazepam was dropped off the nightly list but Quetiapine is retained for one more night. All laxatives were ceased yesterday. It looks as if she could be exiting the medication catacombs!

I told her, again, that she will make a full recovery, as she felt stomped-on by Victoria's pessimistic tone yesterday. Considerable efforts will be required but I do believe in a complete recovery. To help, we will need to access Tamworth's facilities.

There's no word on the transfer: still waiting on a bed in Armidale and reviews here of the lung results.

Thursday, March 27 (day 60)

Morning

Victoria is merely another hurdle Julie has to clear. Meanwhile, she would be happy if her vitality would return and she could eat without feeling sick or having reflux. Otherwise, there is gradual improvement.

I set up music for her to listen to with ear phones. It is a collection of quiet music from our car USB stick, which has many Indian pieces on it. Listening to music should be highly beneficial for her brain recovery (I wonder if they offer that, along with massage, at Ryde and Tamworth). She said to me tonight that it is pleasant but the Indian pieces make her sad. "Because I know I will never be going back to India."

Evening

Julie complains about the slippery elm, and probiotic pills: "Not more sticks to swallow?" Her tummy can only take so much, and that should be food. We are not in a good environment for things like appetisers, which they provided in the Indian hospital. I have to feed her one 'stick' every twenty minutes or her stomach reacts. The slippery elm capsule contents would be better mixed with the yoghurt to coat the oesophagus.

There are a lot of helpful things her friends or I could do in Armidale but here we take small steps. The staff are trying to arrange a wheelchair to take her out of the building, into the sun. She has been stuck inside a hospital room for two months, which emotionally, amounts to years for her. She is almost ready for a wheelchair adventure but her strength must be sufficient to last the distance. It isn't yet. She could manage, though not gain from the experience as she is exhausted by sitting up for too long. However, some days her energy is fine. It is a matter of catching the moment, which is always consumed by the pageant of doctors and what-not that parades in and out every day leaving her drained. Nonetheless, she is becoming stronger, and her consciousness is growing clearer.

I'm sure at this point there is a lot that could naturally draw her forward. Later, we can access the mind exercises the rehab units can offer. It is thought to be more a case of *when* she is ready, rather than whether the time has past for it. This is a different story than the earlier one. Now we're informed that brain injury rehab can only kick-in once she has passed a recovery threshold. Why can't she be in Armidale Hospital then, where she has access to the people who make her feel brighter?

Friday, March 28 (day 61)

Morning

I must admit a correction regarding the mix-up on Julie's chart. There was a good reason that one of her sedative medications was absent from the new chart: Matt had removed it from regular use. The duty doctor added it back on because I felt Julie had endured a bad night previously. Talking with Matt a day later, we agreed it should be removed. This situation reflects my ambiguous role here. I tend to be more of a patient advocate than a spouse, because of Julie's unique condition, but also because of the large number of teams involved.

I sense there is unease within the hospital about this role of mine but I have little choice. There have been so many instances where I had to initiate action from medical staff, to prevent Julie being left in distress. It is also because she constantly requires my presence, as it makes her less fearful. ('Fearfulness means people return to any normality more slowly' wrote psychologist Peter Levine in his book, *In an Unspoken Voice*. It is informative to note that Julie rarely felt fearful while in India. It was only once her left brain resurfaced in POWH that her anxieties manifested. The safety of familiarity really matters after trauma.) But my advocate role is awkward as I comprehend little that is happening, not being consulted in most medical decisions. I have to scramble to keep up.

An example of this is occurring now with our transfer to Armidale. We have been told it will happen but there are medical matters to be dealt with in POWH first. Thus, as this move is delayed and as we haven't seen a doctor for two days, we have no idea what is happening! Tracking down the nurse responsible for room allocations in the ward, I will need to ask her if all we are waiting for is advice from Armidale on room availability. They would prefer us to just trust them, and wait till we are informed. But spending days not knowing what is happening is stressful, especially for Julie as she is in an emotionally sensitive condition. So, once again, I will need to investigate precisely the reasons for this delay.

Julie has reached a turning point in her resurrecting consciousness, where it is critical her choices, decisions, and responses are taken seriously. In certain cases, I leave the room when she is doing things with staff. This is, no doubt, a familiar experience for those recovering in hospital from serious conditions. The physios first suggested this, probably so she couldn't enlist me in her appeals to resist them; also, it increased her return to autonomy. I recognised this as a wise suggestion. Previously, it had been critical for me to be present to interpret, inform and remember, as Julie couldn't do that on her own. Now, I have begun absenting myself whenever a specialist visitor could benefit by not having me around.

More crucially, matching her mental progress, Julie has begun to seek ownership of her recovery. This is an excellent threshold which must be encouraged. I should credit this insight to my friend Dr. Ned Iceton during a conversation at the time – he was wise in this, as in a few other matters.

Evening

Julie is depressed with the endlessness of it all – her condition, and of being at POWH. Yet I feel that things are changing for the better: her strength is growing daily, her mind was clear today (she scored top marks on the PTA test), her stomach problems are abating and she is eating more, with less reflux though still with nausea. The doctors are not concerned about the 'nodules' found in the lung scan, which was a cause for concern a few days ago and not fully explained to us. Now it is less of a problem, so I'm told.

Room availability ostensibly remains the reason for not being transferred to Armidale Hospital. I spoke with the room manager here, who said she contacts Armidale every day. But the truth was revealed by Matt today: Armidale Hospital doctors are 'in discussion' about Julie's admittance. By the end of day Matt had heard nothing. What the issue is I have no idea but hopefully it will be resolved by Monday. On the surface, Julie is close to being out of PTA. She is clear of the multi-resistant CRE bugs, physically stronger and walking quite far now with two physios beside her. By the end of next week she should be toileting independently. Yet she remains in a 'grey area': not completely out of PTA, not classified as clear of the CRE bugs, and still requiring a slow physio program. Personally, I expect she will soon shoot past this dithering!

The wheelchair has arrived. Victoria came by, and in a better mood, although Julie still finds her style rather tiring. She was encouraging about our idea of wheeling outside the room, and I suspect the wheelchair is courtesy of her intercession. But the last word was that we can only travel within the ward (where Julie already walks) and she must be fitted out in plastic gown and gloves. It is hardly what was hoped for but at least we can test out the wheelchair, and maybe even break the rules and descend in the lift.

Saturday, March 29 (day 62)

Morning

Progress is definitely happening, albeit too slowly for Julie's liking. Yesterday, I finally had the reading glasses right. I bought generic magnification glasses from the foyer chemist, tried some, until we found the x3 ones work best. Then I searched the local newsagent for reading material, and found a magazine she might enjoy which has clear text and short articles, of which she read a little. Today, she put the laptop on her lap and read a few emails until she tired. The reflux has abated, and the colic is only an occasional mild upset.

Nausea is preventing her eating but today I bought ginger tablets from the chemist. If those help it will be preferable to asking the nurses for anti-nausea pills. I'll also cut up multivitamin pills, and try a third each day, as she is not taking hospital-supplied supplement drinks – they're too sweet for her.

We did 'wheelchair practice' this afternoon. So there is a lot to be pleased about! Now, all we need is the green light from Armidale Hospital. I hope that won't be another struggle.

Evening

Armidale Hospital has rejected Julie again! They agreed last Tuesday, but this afternoon I was informed that late on Friday they changed their decision. This continuing drama of acceptance and refusal is having a debilitating effect on Julie's mental balance. I don't know what to expect tonight, so I have organised the nurse to administer Quetiapine, and also to request the duty doctor to prescribe Temazepam if Julie wakes distressed during the night. I may have to return if she rings me. She is worried about how much distress her mind can absorb, being unable to control her anxiety levels. She reminded me of a breakdown in her early twenties, and is afraid something similar might happen now.

She is affected both by the constant rejection and by the difficulties with some nurses, like the French guy who didn't comprehend why she has been crying. As well, there's the anticipation of more strange places and people, with no way out. Tonight, I was concerned about her myself, so devoted an intensive healing session on her when I returned to the caravan park after dinner.

On Facebook, my sister Marilyn posted: "Maybe it is time for all of us to put in the same concerted effort with prayers/mind messages that we put in for Julie when she first had her accident and made such an amazing recovery. A combined mental force directed at Armidale Hospital for a change of mind. When reason fails the alternative powers can often succeed."

Sunday, March 30 (day 63)

Morning

Relief! Julie slept soundly through the night and awoke refreshed. She ate breakfast without discomfort. This is an indication that she is healing from the brain trauma: her emotions are stabilising. We will lift our spirits with a cup of tea then break the rules and, with the wheelchair, descend the lift and exit the building... into the sunshine!

Afternoon

We escaped. Down the lift, through the front doors and into the light. What amazed Julie was the scent of sea air. We were encouraged in this escapade by one of the nurses – the French guy! On returning to her room, she slept, while I went to the bakery and brought back a spinach and cheese roll, for which she had been hankering. She not only polished that off with ginger beer but then proceeded to eat most of the curried prawns lunch. All with no ill effects! I had given her three ginger tablets and even breakfast hadn't upset her tummy. There's no stopping her now.

Monday, March 31 (day 64)

Morning

I spoke to two friends who have had close dealings with brain injury rehabilitation. Evidently, NSW is superior to QLD in this matter. The advantage is that in NSW a supervisor coordinates the psychology, physiotherapy, brain rehab and so on. This makes a big difference because, as I am keenly aware, in hospital there are multiple specialist areas which don't necessarily communicate with each other. One is caught in the middle trying to piece it all together.

Both my friends had positive things to say about brain injury rehab. In Julie's case, the lack of a single coordinating person specialised in brain injury is precisely what we don't have, and this is the role I have had to inexpertly scurry around trying to fill. If we were in Tamworth or Ryde, no doubt that role would be competently filled, but we aren't there, and if we were, Julie would still be suffering from disorientation distress. This could be alleviated by being with friends in Armidale. There is no easy solution.

Evening

Julie made a big step forward yesterday. She is eager to advance with rehab, although the fatigue remains annoying. Her mental state on being denied reverting to Armidale is less concerning now than it was a week ago. She would dearly love to be back in Armidale, but ready for whatever direction she is sent now, as long as they get on with it!

The debate about her next move has become a big issue among the nobs in these hospitals. Typical of this whole saga is that Julie has created her own unique identity, and remains an un-slottable item within the system. Even among the nurses she exercises an element which divides the humans from the machines. From my perspective this is due to her uncompromising honesty, whether it be how she is feeling in herself at any time or towards others. She is an un-dismissable person, without even trying. It is fascinating to see the way she draws out the personal in those who deal with her, or else they scamper away. The people she does touch appear genuinely affected in a way they can't quite explain.

Tuesday, April 1 (day 65)

Now the medical head of POW Hospital, Prof Patrick Bolton, has become involved. He had an intensive talk with Warren yesterday. Anything could happen.

Psychologically and emotionally, Julie has reverted to depression. She is on a roller-coaster ride of emotions, telling me she will never leave hospital and wants to die. Often saying, if she had a way to kill herself she would: "I'll stick a knife through my eye!" She let this be known not only to me but also to the nurses and doctors from Rehab. I have not been concerned, as I know her well by now, and her hyperbole when ill is legendary. Nonetheless, I keep our one sharp knife hidden in the room. But this has caused concern from the Rehab psychiatrists, so that Jeff, of the Rehab team, returned to talk with Julie alone this morning.

I stayed outside and worked, while they had a long session. Afterwards, she told me she found it helpful. She assured them she wasn't serious about killing herself – "I'm too much of a coward to kill myself" she told them – but the sentiment is a serious indication of how distressed she is about everything: her health, Armidale Hospital's refusal, the situational stagnation post eye operation, and loneliness in Sydney where she knows almost no one.

Wednesday, April 2 (day 66)

Still no word on a move. I would have expected to hear today if a flight is to happen by Friday, so it's likely we will be here over the weekend. Julie is not happy about the whole thing.

Meanwhile, she continues to improve physically. She typed on the computer for the first time today and browsed Facebook for a while. Her walking is better, and they have allowed me to take her for walks around the ward, when the physios can't make it. Tiredness is now her main obstacle.

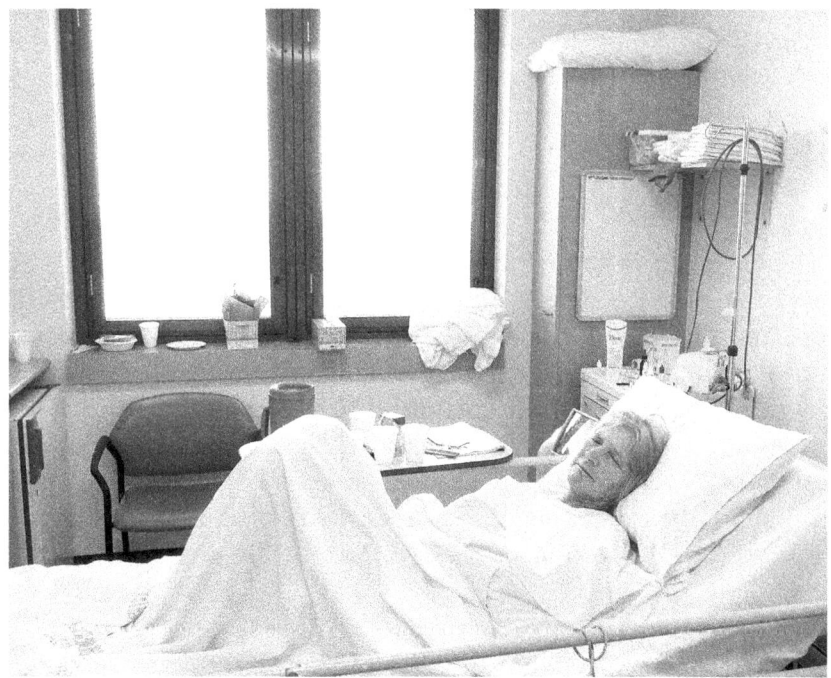

Julie in Price of Wales Hospital

Thursday, April 3 (day 67)

Morning

Just spoke with Matt. Everything possible is being done to transfer Julie out of this acute ward, preferably to Armidale. This is becoming a serious ethical issue between the hospitals. Armidale's refusal to take her back has caused the Eye Clinic to question if they would ever take another patient from Armidale Hospital. The head of POWH is currently still in conversation with Armidale Hospital, and Julie's good progress is helping her case considerably. What exactly is the real issue at Armidale Hospital? Who is the person responsible, and what's their problem?

Meanwhile, Julie is emotionally affected by this stalling. She wanted to type her own message to her friends on Facebook, instead of dictating to me:

"I've been working so hard to improve that itmakes me cry and vomit.They are all very pleaesaithmy progress. abuai'm losing heart. iz'mso sad and lonrly nofeel i'll nrvrt dee home again. sorryforrtyping bu eyesight is stillbad."

Her Facebook friends responded to this with love and support.

Afternoon

Warren rode in to the hospital on his Triumph Bonneville to check Julie's eye. Infection remains but only a small spot now. Possibly the nausea, occasional tummy pains and vertigo, are due to the antifungal medication, Fluconazole. This antifungal is still seen as a low toxicity medication, so it's a detriment-benefit case and the benefit remains substantial.

The big news he had for us was that Victoria had written on Julie's record that she no longer requires neuro-rehab. Victoria has come good, and provided the one essential piece of the puzzle! I presume it can only be because Julie has been performing satisfactorily in her daily PTA tests. This makes a critical difference to the case for returning to Armidale Hospital as it removes their rationale for denying acceptance. "Well done Victoria", or perhaps I should say, Julie. I'm sure Victoria based her change of assessment on sound evidence from Julie's regular PTA testing.

The Hospital Ordeal

Many who have suffered through the hospital system travail will immediately recognise the frustration we endured throughout this period. Julie's unique condition emphasised the structural deficiencies in the system. Jeff, the 'fix-it' man from Rehab, who first acknowledged that the hospital was not coping with her case management, only served to reify our feelings of confusion and exasperation. We certainly need the expertise of specialities that only the hospital system can provide. But in the midst of the hustle and bustle of medical procedures, we desperately strove to sustain a belief that the pinprick of light in this dark tunnel would grow into a doorway to the sunlight of our own life.

It was this, that no medical staff person could offer us, or even acknowledge. We were human, with all the emotional, aspirational and unique personal worlds that entails. There was no section of the hospital responsible for that, from which we could draw comfort or advocacy. We were trapped in a machine, dedicated to the body, not the soul.

On top of which, we were aware of struggles within the system to accommodate Julie's complex needs, without the recognition that they were playing with the precipitous psychological extremes of a brain trauma condition. Jeff's arrival was the first time anyone from the machine of the hospital system had taken the time to include Julie or me in the incomprehensible algorithms of decision.

He listened, made notes, offered sympathies and yet he still left into the hospital wilderness to 'report' to ... who? Like every other specialist that appeared in Julie's room for whatever conceivable reason – out they went and never a word heard back. The Rehab psychiatrist, whose assessment mysteriously hung over us as a high court judgement, never asked us to review or participate in that which persisted, even months later, as a final, uncontested, pessimistic pronouncement on Julie's status.

I passed him in the corridor on my way to lunch one day, and had the overwhelming desire to grab him by the neck and shout, "Excuse me! We are human beings and we want a say in all these fucking secret decisions you make about our lives!" But I didn't – just watched him turn into one of those endless doorways through which 'staff only' were allowed or even knew about. It was a consolation to discover a long time later that his prognosis was completely wrong. Ironically, he was a doctor of Indian origin.

The system had us by the balls and our only recourse was to play by their rules, watching like a python for the slivers of hope that accidently passed our eyes. I contained my anger and used it skilfully.

Our life-line was always the wonderful Eye Clinic registrars, yet we felt they were as impotent in the drama that raged above us between hospitals on the rarefied management level. I can't blame anyone – it is just the nature of the battle for survival between the personal and the organisation behemoth. We fared better than many, and Julie often wondered with dread how she would have coped on her own.

Friday, April 4 (day 68)

Morning

Previously, I had mentioned to Julie's Facebook friends my lack of knowledge of the current political incumbents for our local area, as we had been away so long. My sister Marilyn, and Wendy, a friend of Julie's, brought up the issue again in our online discussions. I felt too remote from these politicians, although Marilyn did remind me that hospitals were a State responsibility, so the State Member of Parliament was the correct person to ask for assistance. Then Wendy gave me his phone number and explained that she had experienced good results from contacting the previous State MP.

After finishing breakfast and dressing, while sitting in the van ready to leave the caravan park, I decided to act. We had nothing to lose and everything to gain if our local MP, Adam Marshall, was able or willing to help. So I rang him.

Adam's office assistant Lisa Williams answered, at first dryly stating I would need to send a request in writing. When, slightly emotionally, I explained that would not be possible for this situation's time frame, she asked for the 'short version'. By the time I had finished, she was highly engaged (she said it sounded like a good film script!) She contacted Adam, who was currently out of town. Lisa explained to me they would be able to deal directly with the office of the minister responsible for hospitals, so avoiding involvement with the conflicting parties – an excellent approach. Later, she informed me they had contacted the State Minister of Health's DLO (Departmental Liaison Officer) on the matter, in addition to the CEO of Hunter New England Health, of which Armidale Hospital is a branch. That sounded pretty good to me! She thought I would hear from them soon.

They are in an excellent position now to help resolve this, because of the new status Julie has reached of no longer requiring neuro-rehab. I must say I have been astounded at her improved mental clarity, even since last Sunday.

Late Morning

The dam has burst, in a big way! I received a phone call from Max Mansoor, the director of Armidale Hospital Medical Services. In short, they are ready, and only require the Nursing Unit managers to conduct the handover. The involvement of our local member could be the only reason they contacted me personally in this whole thing. Thanks to Marilyn and Wendy for the details – I'd only needed a little push, and the timing was ripe. At last!

I had been in Julie's room when the Ward Social Worker asked to speak with me, for a change. Apparently the doctors were concerned about how I was coping, as all the attention had been on Julie. Jeff had earlier asked if I had spoken with the Social Workers for my own benefit, and I'd told him I was fine. But he must have alerted them to check.

The social worker was a pleasant young woman. So many of the POWH staff are eager young people, with loads of training but little life experience. I like them, and find their naive manners refreshing. We went into a separate room where we could talk without interruption. She apologised for this being so late in the phase, as Julie was under the Eye Clinic, not the Infectious Ward itself. Always more than happy to chat away, I ran through my side of things, although telling her I was generally capable of handling most demands that came my way.

During our talk, the call from Max came on my phone. He, and another person in his office, on speaker phone, explained they'd been working for the last three days tying up the requirements and conditions of Julie's transfer. And, I reflected, the credit must really go to the efforts of Patrick Bolton, Director of Clinical Medical Services, Prince of Wales Hospital, who has been striving all week to resolve the impasse with Armidale Hospital.

The effusive friendliness from Max made me smile, for it was truly appreciated in contrast to the sense of abandonment and rejection we had been feeling for the last two weeks. Max was excellent in explaining the details, and offering his mobile number for me to contact, even over the weekend. That was a refreshing change in mood for us. To feel welcome in returning, rather than begrudgingly accepted, is important for Julie, being sensitive to these things.

While I was explaining the good news to Julie, Patrick Bolton himself came into the ward, and I was sorry not to go out from the room to meet him, but Julie had to come first. Warren also turned up in his leather riding jacket – this was his day off but he wasn't going to miss the excitement. He spent the next three hours at the computer finalising our discharge papers then came in to say goodbye. Julie was sorry to see him go – she felt, in different circumstance, we could have been good friends. She was smitten with him and his curly red hair!

Certainly, the key to this was Victoria's reclassification of the neuro-rehab status for Julie. It is funny how that turned around, but it has been typical of those who have been dealing with her. I'm sure Patrick Bolton's efforts laid the groundwork for the details of the transfer, but I'm under no illusions that Adam Marshall, via Lisa Williams, lit the bomb under the seats of those who had been delaying things.

Julie was finally accepted into Armidale Hospital by Dr. Nihal Nanda, a doctor originally from South India, which was appropriate in the circumstance. They have secured the outpatient consultations of the head of the Tamworth Brain Injury Unit – also welcome news.

She will fly out around noon tomorrow! How it could happen that quickly, and on a weekend, is another mystery most likely connected to Adam Marshall's efforts. But we'll need to see if the departure follows through so soon. Tony will be there to meet her at Armidale Hospital, as I won't be able to drive back in time. Julie is so delighted, to put it mildly! Now we re-cock our readiness for the next phase.

Return to Armidale Hospital

Saturday. April 5 (day 69)

Night

Julie, relieved, was returned to Armidale Hospital. Tony came to visit, then our ever-loyal friends Christine and Lyla Stephen, making her feel welcomed and 'at home'. I arrived about 7pm following a long seven hour drive, in time to see Julie before she dropped off to sleep. She is in an excellent room, looking out a full-wall window to the treed hills of the town's south; this is a comfort, as she was so unhappy in POWH with no sight of the sky or trees.

But there was something I slipped up on. In this business, one has to look ahead for all possible mishaps. You would think the flight attendants who took Julie away on a stretcher would transfer her horizontally into the plane. Mistake. No, they suggested she climb unaided up the steps to board! Based on her recent confidence with the POWH physios, and feeling she must be independent, she agreed. But I should have thought to ensure they knew she couldn't walk unassisted. She had been walking so finely, needing only one person now, to steady her. But not up aeroplane steps on her own!

She fell at the first step. They were very nice, she told me (so they should have been) and finally lay her on a stretcher and into the plane. After that, she lost confidence and couldn't walk to the bathroom at the hospital without a lot of support. She should be better tomorrow but it shows that every little possibility has to be anticipated. And there I was thinking it would be easier back in Australia.

Sunday, April 6 (day 70)

Julie was thrilled to receive a posy of yellow roses from her friend Mabs. Softly gold and bright, they had the best aroma of any roses, ever! It's only the first day in Armidale, and Julie feels much more relaxed and happy. Tomorrow, Monday, the medical processes will begin, which will be interesting. The nurses tell me that about six weeks stay in hospital is predicted; I'm glad of that time, for the intensive physio Julie will require before returning home. Day trips to home or into town will be allowed once she becomes foot-steady. Even before that I'm sure we can exit the hospital in the wheelchair but she is in such a beautiful room, with a full view of the South Hill trees, that the need to 'escape' is not so pressing. She is also glad that the nurses relate personally here, and it is quieter than POWH.

I am happy to be home, and there is plenty to do. Finally, a return to normal routines: the poultry, our dear twenty-two year old cranky cat Sheena, the washing, cooking, gardening, mowing, tax returns. And the Tour of Flanders cycling is on tonight!

Tuesday, April 8 (day 72)

Julie has been delighted with the flowers that have arrived in her room. She is also pleased to see those friends who have been able to visit – it's uplifting for her, and not as tiring as it was last time here. There had been a problem in the past with too many people being in the room, exhausting her brain, but this week she has been appreciating the visitors which indicates a big change in her energy – she is coming out of PTA quickly. Her slow rate of healing progress still annoys her as does the occasional unsympathetic nurse, but in all, they are perceptive and efficient here at Armidale Hospital. I'm impressed.

Her new physician doctor-in-charge, Dr. Nihal Nanda, originally from Hyderabad, India, is also impressive. He is astute and competent. He even used the word 'holistic' in his confirmation of Julie's need to return to Armidale for her neuro-healing. We had a good chat about Indian politics and the medical quality in South India.

I'm still trying to find the best arrangement for Julie to use her computer. At present, being in the armchair might work but she hates sitting because it make her feel unwell. She also develops a pain somewhere in her bottom while sitting, which could be bruising of the coccyx bone. Much testing of different chairs and cushions is going on but she prefers to be in bed.

Friday, April 11 (day 75)

The local ophthalmologist, Dr. Mark Morgan, has administered eye drops that have impaired Julie's vision, though he explained the effect should clear in three days. This causes her difficulty in reading text and typing on the computer. Still, Mark is happy with the recovery of her left eye; better vision should soon return. A new glasses prescription will be necessary but magnification glasses will suit for the time being. Overall, she's improving, and can see the photos from our India trip pasted along the wall. Some of these were on the wall in Sydney but I've had a new set made up. She enjoys them, as they create a good talking point with visitors and are happy memories. We steer away from the unhappy ones. She is uncomfortable when the conversation comes around to the hotel fire. It is not time to deal with that yet.

Thursday, April 17 (day 81)

Julie has progressed amazingly since our return, and is walking independently with only an attendant to lend confidence, and support her if she falters. Today, for the first time, she was sitting in the chair with her laptop on the table. If the nurse hadn't come in to do her 'Obs' (observations), and spent so long over that, she would have engaged with her emails and Facebook. Eventually, with all the fuss over the difficulty with her Obs, she became tired. It was unfortunate they had come at that time. Mark Morgan visited this morning and is pleased with her left eye, which continues to improve. She will be on the anti-fungal medication for at least another two weeks though.

So many of Julie's friends have dropped by, with flowers, food, large-print books which she has enjoyed, and simple affectionate companionship, which she has been so happy to share. Outside or home-made food is a big help as she has become jaded by hospital meals. We exited the building in the wheelchair last weekend, and I'll try that again over the Easter break. If it's sunny, maybe we'll even have something better for lunch on the garden seats.

Dr. Nanda has been excellent, and he hands back to Dr. Braslins next week. Dr. Braslins is one of the new heads of the University of New England Medical School, as well as Julie's primary hospital doctor. There is a curious connection there for me, due to my involvement in development of the Joint Medical School's management database. Dr. Nanda will be back in two weeks. Julie is fond of him, and impressed, feeling safe and reassured by his presence, his way of connecting. When asked about trauma counselling he explained that Julie needed to be out of PTA before counsellors become involved. She has to remember what the counsellor says, one of the nurses added. That sounds reasonable, although it wouldn't have been much use had I settled for such an approach all this time. Instead, I have been adopting the old method of patient repetition, over and over. Anyway, she is classified as being out of PTA now, and the daily tests have ceased.

The brain injury team from Tamworth Base Hospital visited Julie during the week. Over time they can do a lot to help her, which I must phone them to discuss. Next Wednesday, the occupational therapists will visit our home to recommend necessary modifications. Railings need to be added here and there, and a few danger spots repaired around the house.

The outside time-frame for her discharge from hospital is five to six weeks but it depends on her progress. Perhaps it could be sooner, as she is growing stronger and more capable every day. Before that time, day trips home and to friends' places will be allowed, which will be fun. In two weeks, I expect to see enough improvement in her capabilities that these day trips could become possible.

She is bored, as expected. She has a radio, books, audio-books, TV and visitors from hospital staff and friends, but she would like to begin writing – she has plenty to say! Unfortunately, the TV doesn't always work properly, so I have to reach up to switch it off and on again. This is too difficult for Julie as it is high on the wall, so I ensure it is working before leaving in the evening. When it stops at other times, the nurses are too busy for these technical adjustments, so she goes without, and doesn't mind. She can't concentrate for long anyway.

Saturday, April 19 (day 83)

Easter Saturday morning: Michael and Phillipa came, and we wheeled Julie down in the lift, through the hospital doors, and out into a little sitting area to enjoy the warm sun with Joan and Carl who turned up, taking tea with a home-prepared Easter lunch. We discovered that if using a special hospital cushion with our own wheelchair she could sit longer before her coccyx began hurting. It was so pleasant to have our friends around, outside the hospital rooms and corridors.

Saturday, May 3 (day 97)

Julie on Facebook: "Happiness! I've been doing so well with rehab and was devastated to develop a very sore eye (my important 'operated on' one) and was worried. But dear Dr. Nanda came this morning and pronounced it is 'something' rhinitis and it will wear off. What joy! The relief! Now M is here, we are about go for a walk (I'm a champion walker, except I always fall to the left). Takes great concentration and occasionally much fear! M is then heading home to put more batts in the ceiling. It's turned cold here."

Tuesday, May 6 (day 100)

Julie on Facebook: "Latest boring health update is that I have to go back to Prince of Wales hospital in Sydney for an operation to put a plate between my brain and my left ear. Disappointing development!"

I had become concerned that Julie's vertigo was hindering her progress, recalling her left ear problems and the advice at POWH, that she should see an ENT specialist when back in Armidale. While in Sydney, when we alerted the doctors to her left ear hearing problems, they had brought in an ENT registrar to examine her. He explained that the ear was full of fluid and needed draining. They were going to do it at the same time as the eye operation but his ENT boss cancelled that, fearing it could introduce infection. Julie was still classified as highly contagious and vulnerable due to her compromised immune system.

On discussing with the doctors in Armidale Hospital that the fluid in Julie's inner ear could be causing balance problems, they booked her into the local ENT specialist, Dr. Peter Macarthur. We managed the trip to his rooms in a wheelchair taxi, and I wheeled her back to the hospital along the footpaths – a good sign that she can manage longer outings in the wheelchair. After examining her ear, Dr. Macarthur pronounced she needed major surgery to seal the fractured tegmen tympani bone, which was leaking cerebrospinal fluid (CSF) into her ear. Pathogens could be introduced through the ear drum, or from the canal that runs to the back of the throat, and once the inner ear becomes infected it can pass into the brain via the fracture.

Julie was annoyed at yet another crisis she had to battle through. "We'll just leave it!" she said. Whereupon he replied, "You could die from this." Oh well, here we go again. Back to POWH in Sydney, to the ENT specialist for a major brain operation in the same area damaged in the fall. There's nothing we can do about it.

We bolster ourselves for a second big trip to Sydney. I was especially stressed by this, having previously become increasingly strained by anxiety for Julie, from having so little exercise, and from living on salty restaurant food. Only just returning to a sense of wellness myself, now we both have to endure this all again. Despite an earlier comment to the Social Worker about my customary imperviousness to any situation, I was beginning to push the limits. My blood pressure had been reading high since returning from Sydney, and rest was needed, with less constant concern and demand upon my energy. I was not going to get it.

Return to Prince of Wales Hospital, Sydney

Friday, May 9 (day 103)

Night

Julie was flown out of Armidale around midday. Dr. Nanda has classified her condition as emergency, based on Dr. Macarthur's assessment. This means she will be treated quickly. We have no idea what this operation will be, but ostensibly, surgery involves entering the skull behind the ear to find and fix the fractured tegmen tympani bone, sealing off the brain.

Dr Nanda was surprised at Dr. Macarthur's assessment, as he thought that if there was a chance of developing meningitis it would have happened long ago. Researching on the Web indicated to me that if meningitis is going to happen it usually occurs in the first seven days post-trauma. Thus, I tended to agree with Dr. Nanda and was not in a panic about the risk of brain infections. Still, it was concerning what a major operation would mean, how Julie would handle another stay at POWH, and once again, how long it would take.

By now, before bed, I am exhausted from organising everything for another trip which could extend indefinitely. Also, I am preparing the house and Sheena, our old Siamese cat, for my absence. Thankfully, my friend Dominic has kindly agreed to house-sit while I am in Sydney. He isn't due to arrive for a few days, so I have engaged the assistance of our helpful neighbour, Rick, to feed Sheena.

Saturday, May 10 (day 104)

Night

I didn't leave home until 11am this morning, as there's so much to finalise. But it was a good trip down from the Northern Tablelands. I enjoy driving, and the road to Sydney via the short-cut of Gloucester is a beautiful route until reaching the highway near Newcastle. Then it's a busy, enervating, and dangerous passage for hours on the freeway to Sydney, heading into the centre of the city at peak hour, trusting solely on the SatNav. I arrived at the hospital after dark and found Julie in a different ward but near one of her previous rooms. She was in reasonable spirits, so I was reassured, although I knew she also was fearful of what a major brain operation would mean.

I was able to buy food from the noodle shops in Randwick centre, a short walk away, where I had eaten so often on our previous stay at POWH. Then I made my way to the caravan park only to find someone in my booked spot, once again! It is a nice caravan park but so many times I've arrived back late to find another van in my allotted space. I was able to squeeze in between two vans, and waited for the usurper to return. When he came, I went to speak with him. He was from Tasmania, and blamed me for his being in my spot! He also blamed Sydney-siders for their pushy arrogance. One meets all types in caravan parks. That is another of the constant side events that have to be negotiated while focusing on the main issue of Julie's medical saga.

Sunday, May 11 (day 105)

Morning

Julie on Facebook: "Guess what! I don't have to have this scary operation! Instead, the ENT Dr. came and manipulated my head so the crystals will go to the right place. I can go back to Armidale (hope they have a bed available)."

I arrived while Dr. Kertesz was examining Julie's ear. He took me to a computer and showed me the CT scan of her head, taken when she was in POWH last time. He pointed to the tegmen tympani bone fracture, comparing it to the 'good' right side. It was easy to see a long latitudinal fracture through which, he said, the cerebrospinal fluid was seeping from the brain to the middle ear.

He explained that he had never seen a case of the tegmen tympani bone not healing on its own. He commented that this kind of fracture was rare for local ENT specialists but they see a lot of such cases at POWH. The important thing is that there has been no leakage from the ear drum. "If that had been the case" he said, "Julie would very likely have contracted meningitis long before now." While the middle ear continues to pool the fluid, it will act as a blockage to further seepage, thus enabling the bone to heal. Seepage inhibits the bone healing process. Thus, they will not drain the ear yet.

We were extremely relieved to hear the recommendation against surgery. I asked him, though, how it would have been done, and he pointed to the area of her skull through which they would have had to dig to access the bone. I was exceedingly happy this was off the agenda!

Next, I asked about her dizziness, which had initiated this whole line of enquiry in Armidale, whether the ear condition could be causing her vertigo problems. "That's a different matter," he said "we'll fix that now." He went back to Julie and performed what he called the Epley technique, for a condition known as BPPV (benign paroxysmal positional vertigo), where crystals detach from the inner ear and become lodged in a section of the semi-circular canals, thus disturbing the fine balance-hairs that reside there.

Dr. Kertesz commented, "Perhaps there's a reason for your coming all this way after all." Why no one in Armidale had suggested this technique, I don't know: he said Julie should start to feel better within about three of four days. So that was a bonus. Let's hope this proves correct!

Julie on Facebook: "But coming down in the air ambulance, to stop myself worrying I remembered Bill Bailey in "Black Books" lying in hospital reading "The Little Book of Calm". Made me happy; I love those actors."

Night

My own health is becoming increasingly disturbing to me. I brought the blood pressure monitor with me, and registering repeated high readings. Tonight my BP was 190/100. In fact it was initially 210/110 but the first reading is always questionable. What to do? The last thing we needed now was for me to have a stroke or heart attack. I am certainly feeling off – there is a buzzing, fast vibration in my body. Should I pack up and admit myself to the POWH Emergency? How high can BP go before it becomes dangerous? I had no idea. Finally, the best choice was to go to sleep and reconsider in the morning – fingers crossed it would be all right.

Monday, May 12 (day 106)

Morning

My BP was down from last night, thank God, but still high. The diastole was back to the normal range of below 80 but the systole was up in the 150s. Perhaps the constant worry surrounding Julie, having almost no exercise for months, and the salty restaurants food, is taking its toll on my typically impervious constitution. I did have a strange sweat-free fever during the night, so perhaps a weird virus is affecting my BP readings. A doctor's appointment is scheduled on returning to Armidale, and he will have received my recent blood tests by now. If I live that long, more answers will be forthcoming.

Night

Julie was flown out to Armidale about 7pm. Thankfully, the hospital there had a room available. I will drive up tomorrow.

Armidale Hospital for third time

Wednesday, May 14 (day 108)

Julie on Facebook: "I'm back at Armidale Hospital, so different from the city one, and next week I am having an excursion home (our home) with the occupational therapist; the beginning of the end of this hospital time! Also I am now allowed to walk alone with the walker, which means I can exercise more and importantly take myself to the loo!!"

Her dizziness has decreased markedly, so the Epley technique has worked. Researching on the Web I found it looks relatively easy for me to perform once she returns home, which hopefully is not far off.

There is a new registrar, Lucy Cochran, who handles the immediate care for Julie in hospital. She is a delightful and bright young doctor, whom we both like and feel confident with. She nips in to see Julie every now and then and relays our concerns to Dr. Braslins or Dr. Nanda. It's so refreshing to have a personable doctor attending.

Yesterday I saw my own doctor, Brian Glover. By then my BP had reverted to its more usual range, around 130/70. Brian said my blood tests were fine – there was nothing wrong with me. Even my cholesterol, which had been creeping up before we left for India, was right down. The Indian vegetarian diet works wonders on cholesterol! When I asked about the BP, he explained one has to have a long period of high BP before it becomes a risk. "How high can it go in any temporary period?" I asked. He explained if it was up into the high 200's one might be in trouble. But my BP had been consistently in the typical range for my age for years, so I had nothing to worry about. That was a reprieve. I had been considering my life was on a precipice a few days ago, and now it appears I'm as strong as a bull. Just more fluctuations on this whole epic since the accident in Trichy.

Saturday, May 17 (day 111)

It has been a big day for Julie and me! I took her in the VW van for a trip around town. This was the first time she had been properly out of hospital, in our car – like old times. During the week, the physio,

Bahao Joo, had brought her to the car for trial runs at climbing in and out of the front or back seats. Bahao has been doing impressive work with Julie to help her walk, handling steps and limb movements. Much of her progress throughout these weeks was due to his excellent and patient sessions. This first car trip was a test in preparation for coming home on a trial run with the occupational therapists (OTs). Julie was still experiencing pains when sitting for too long, and nausea on occasion, so we needed to know she could make the half-hour trip home along winding roads. She enjoyed the sights as we drove around the Autumn-leafed streets of Armidale. It was one step closer to coming home for good!

Another person Julie is having extra help from is the nurse Bernadette Foster. Bernie is attached to the physio team, so she has a lot to do with rehab progress. Bernie has been at Armidale Hospital for a long time, and remembers our mutual friends who went through nursing training with her, decades ago. Bernie was able to comfort Julie in times when she became distressed at her apparent unchanging disabilities. Julie continues to have emotional lows but in general, she is fond of the hospital and its staff. It has become her home, and she is nervous at the thought of leaving for our home out of town, where she will only have me to assist.

Monday, May 19 (day 113)

I collected Julie today in the van and brought her home, with the OTs following, to test whether she could cope with house situations like the shower, the steps, chairs and so forth. Although this was a 'business' trip – a functional procedure to check that everything is in place – nonetheless, for both of us it was a major event. This was the first time she had been home in eight months.

It was looking beautiful. Autumn leaves glowed on the trees, the open fire flickered in the lounge room, the sun shone in the crisp afternoon. I had been working hard to finish all the modifications. With the help of our friend Gerard Stephen, one of the owners of this huge pastoral property that has been our home for decades, and also aided by our trusty neighbour Rick, we had installed railings on the steps and in the shower. Rick and I had dug up half the path leading to the main entrance, and laid new cement. I created two pretty rangolis (Indian blessing patterns) on the path in front of the gate and door, using rice flower and rangoli stencils we bought on our trip through India.

There were so many times in hospital, especially in Sydney, that Julie felt she would never see her home and garden again, nor her dear old cat, Sheena. I brought Sheena to visit her one day in hospital but now finally, she was able to see her at home. I had kept assuring Julie she would get home again – not to worry – and now, it was happening. It was an important moment for us albeit crimped by the functionality of the kind OTs. We understood. They have to do their job. I felt, nonetheless, that the home-coming was lit up by the same presence that had shielded Julie throughout her ordeal. It could easily have been a freezing, wet day, of which we've had many recently. Instead, it was a picturesque reception, for someone who has struggled valiantly through a plethora of physical and emotional sufferings. It was a sign to me that my intent of a full recovery would eventuate.

Thursday, May 29 (day 123)

Julie left hospital on a day pass, to visit the optometrist. It was critical she obtain new prescription glasses, as her previous ones were now unsuitable for both her eyes. During the examination of her current vision status, the optometrist said she had 6/6 vision in her left eye (20/20 in the old measurement). We were both astounded! I admit to not having been confident she would regain vision in the vitrectomy eye, so this was a welcome outcome. Still, Julie was seeing more clearly today, which has not been the case every day. But if she could achieve 6/6 vision once, it is most probable that, over time, it will stabilise at that level. It was one more miracle in a long list of miracles throughout this saga.

Identity

I walked into the hospital one day while Julie was in conversation with Carol Gregory, the speech therapist. Carol was another person on the hospital staff doing excellent work to help Julie regain her mental capacities. Julie was highly impressed with her sessions. Carol asked me if I thought Julie had changed since the accident. "Yes," I replied, "she is more child-like." I had been pondering something for a long time during this marathon recovery, and gradually had come to the conclusion that she really did die in that fall from the hotel window in Trichy. But it was no coincidence, as her life had markedly changed over the years prior to the accident.

Her mother, to whom she had been devoted and constantly attended for five years following a stroke, had died a year before we left on the Indian trip. We had wound up her mother's affairs, including preparing and selling her house, so that by the time we left, Julie had folded a huge tome of her life. As an academic historian, she had completed a current research job at the University of New England. A whole life-phase of her identity had concluded. Our journey to India this time was as much a deserved break, and a long-awaited adventure, as a conscious demarcation of her life – a journey for renewal and rediscovery of who she is now and who she will be for the remainder of her physical life. We hadn't anticipated it unfolding in such a dramatic way.

We had woven our way through the narrow alleyways and packed crowds of Old Delhi's Chandni Chowk, walked among the scented forests of deodar cedar and Himalayan oak in Landour, awoken to visions of the snow-gleaming Nanda Devi mountain streaming through our bedroom window at Kasar Devi in the Kumaon hills, made offerings in the ancient stone shrines of Jageshwar, and strolled in the crisp autumn air around the beautiful lake of Nainital. Julie had (once again) nearly died through sickness in the timeless 'city of death', Varanasi, recovering just in time to witness the fabulous light explosions of Devdiwali from a boat on the river Ganga. We had climbed high to the temple of Anjaneya in Hampi and looked out upon a boulder-strewn landscape of the once magnificent city of Vijayanagar, watched thrilling

Indian Classical music concerts hosted by the Maharaja of Travancore in Trivandrum, and celebrated Christmas with the Syrian Christians of Fort Cochin in the typical, colourful style of India. We had luxuriated on the beach of Kovalam where we met friends from previous visits, spent days looking out through the mists from our room's verandah at Kodaikanal over the precipitous escarpment into the Cumbum Valley, six thousand feet below. We'd soaked in the sacred atmosphere of one of the most moving temples of the world, the great granite-carved Brihadishvara Temple of Thanjavur. By the time of our meeting with destiny at Trichy, we were at ease and enjoying ourselves within the Indian milieu, which is saying a lot, because India is surely one of the most challenging countries in the world in which to travel. And the hotel fire itself had come completely out of the blue – an 'act of God' as is said in the insurance industry, with no question of likely risk, or anticipated danger. In a matter of moments, something totally unexpected turned our lives a complete somersault. It was as if we had climbed a great metaphorical mountain to a high cliff ledge, then jumped off!

That Julie survived this fall was a miracle. That she continued to survive through the long journey of recovery, crawling inch by inch out of the dark labyrinths of illness, was an even greater miracle. This accident revealed the changes which experiences through India had wrought upon her soul, quietly and indelibly beneath the surface.

As we were travelling south from Goa, along the Karavali Coast of India, we realised we were heading into the 'comfort zone' of Kerala, which was more about relaxation and enjoyment than the challenging adventures of new places. One day, Julie mentioned to me that while entering this last and easiest part of our trip, she still hadn't resolved the questions of identity and purpose that had so preoccupied her mind. By now though, it was dawning on me that she had altered substantially through this journey. So much had happened, such highlights and depths, joys and hardships, that without fully realising it, she had become a different person. The accident in Trichy was, in fact, only the culmination of this transformation: a destiny that was always waiting for us, a passageway to a new and incomprehensible life.

Her fall, the subsequent injuries and hospitalization, including the extreme emotional anxieties she weathered during her recovery, acted like the distillation of alcoholic spirits. An essence was refined which contained two threads: an artless personality, and a strength – a sense of certitude that I had never observed in Julie before. This potency was a consequence of the Indian journey, developing before the accident.

And the guileless qualities, probably came from what I perceived as a death and rebirth through the accident itself.

Within the first few days in the ICU of GVN Hospital, I recognised the companion I knew so well. By the second week, this Julie had disappeared. But its initial appearance clarified for me, from the first time she spoke, that everything quintessentially Julie was still functioning. A serious brain injury, as she had suffered, can sever neurological threads, sharply altering a person's capacity and personality. From the earliest point, I realised that that type of damage had not occurred. But there was another kind of character shift, which took me a long while to comprehend, and for her, will take many years to unfold.

The 'new Julie' that manifested in the second week of ICU was an instinctive one. Psychologically, I felt I was dealing with her as a newly born baby. She reacted with spontaneous instinct to every situation while retaining, on another level, her mental clarity and self-reflective abilities. This was fascinating and surprising for me to witness. It was both complex and highly simplified, at the same time. As the weeks and months passed, Julie's personality developed like a child growing older, and despite retaining her insightful and sophisticated mentality, she maintained a direct and unaffected honesty. Gone was the self-interest, interpretative interface through which adults filter their world. In its place was an unaffected spontaneity only seen in children. Oddly, it was this quality that appeared to attract and win over many of the nurses and doctors we encountered throughout the hospitalization process. Even those she was abusing (like the physios) couldn't help be attracted to her emotional honesty – it was refreshing, in a world of spin and connivance.

The strength Julie manifested through the long Indian experience was also intriguing for me to observe. Gone were her previous traits of uncertainty and deference-to-the-world. India doesn't have time for dithering: if you don't grab your space someone else will. They don't bother with the polite niceties commonly expected in our own societal intercourse. Life is too immediate, intense, and the safety nets that underpin our luxuries of sham-courteousness don't exist in India. The individual is not so important there; you just get on with life and take what you need. When I had been away procuring food at night across the city in Trichy, I had often been concerned that Julie was lonely and worried back in her hospital room, yet when I returned, there she would be, lying in bed perfectly centred and at ease. She became stressed from pain or disorientation, especially when back in Australia, but that was a different issue. It never undermined her new persona, one which now knew who she was on a deep level, and was comfortable with that knowledge – like a person who had finally found themselves after a lifetime of looking in all the wrong places. She had found a personal home within.

This change manifested noticeably in the last month in Armidale Hospital. Julie was at home in her hospital room, especially in bed. She had worked out the functional aspects of living in hospital. She knew the names of all the staff, and interacted with them both on a personal and practical level. She managed the little peripheral features of life, such as the table, the food, the room cleaning, the clothing changes, the TV, the phone, the physiotherapy sessions with the always-pleasant-and-attentive Bahao, and the visits from Susan Elms of the Tamworth Brain Injury unit, who was to take over consulting for the post-hospital rehabilitation phase. Julie had it all in hand, within her limited physical abilities.

She came to know the personal lives of many of the staff, and took an interest in other patients she encountered. By the time she was ready to leave, she had settled in at hospital. This is perhaps a common experience of many long-term patients but I could see something different in Julie: she was at home in her room because she was at home in herself. She was often depressed and distressed at her lack of recovery, or irritated with me and the staff for various reasons, yet that never dislodged this vision I constantly had of her being centred within herself. She could be happy or sad, but the innocent, unaffected directness, married with her strength and certitude into a fresh identity whose potential was yet to be realised. This was the new journey she had now begun – who was this person, and what would she do with it?

Friday, May 30 (day 124)

My last post to Julie's Facebook page:

> "Julie was discharged this afternoon, and is home, asleep in her own bed, at last.
>
> On Wednesday she went to the optometrist who proclaimed her left eye now has 20/20 vision. After everything that has happened to it, this is amazing. There are still residual things to follow up, such as her fractured tegmen tympani bone, which the ENT specialist in POWH says will heal of its own accord. We will travel to Sydney in a month for a check-up. But on the whole, Julie is well on her way to a complete recovery. She is still wobbly on her pegs, her muscles are sore from exercises, and she tires quickly

but every week she is gaining strength. We'll have to start planning our next trip soon!

Thank you all for the help and support you provided to us both during this whole epic. I personally found it invaluable. I'll be signing off now — Julie can handle the computer well enough, and she should have her new glasses in a week."

As expected, it was not the end of this epic. Julie's rehab had only begun. There was a long journey of slow yet steady recovery ahead. But at last, she had exited the doors of the hospital system, and was home. That was a huge relief, after visualising this day so many times in my healing sessions almost every night since that fateful day in Trichy. Often, I was unable to allow myself to speak of the trust that this would turn out to be one of those incredible experiences one looked back upon, as a great story of self-discovery. I was too seriously worrying that Julie would not survive. But in the back of my mind, I never gave up trusting in a strange power that constantly found ways through every insurmountable obstacle. And now Julie had walked out of the subterranean tunnels, into the sunny fresh air: truly a miracle.

Epilogue

Julie was discharged from the hospital system and had returned home, but that was only the beginning of the next chapter of her recovery, which was to be an exceedingly long journey. The path to full recovery was not only to pass through repeated crises, but also to begin an understanding of what 'recovery' meant for her. The statements she made during her time in Prince of Wales Hospital, that she was saddened by listening to Indian music because she knew she would never return there, laid down the trajectory of this next phase of recovery: to revisit India!

Julie walked out of hospital in mid-2014. There was no point in planning a return to India that summer, as it was obviously too soon – she was still frail. But to gain the benefit of our frequent-flyer credits we need to reserve seats a year ahead. We booked, in a mood of unrealistic optimism, for the summers of 2015 and 2016, only to cancel both times. On the third attempt, the summer of 2017, we succeeded, but there was a long and difficult struggle to finally reach that goal.

The first drama to assail Julie, post-hospitalization, was that she became progressively weaker. Not only that but her hair was falling out. The hair loss was distressing but the physical weakness was a serious situation. Subsequent to long hospitalization, she was debilitated, and desperately needed to rebuild strength, especially as that was a major component of her balance recovery. Without which, she was in danger of falling. Aside from breaking bones, which would incapacitate her for another long stretch, she risked hitting her head and becoming more permanently disabled.

Julie was frustrated by this developing condition, and I was concerned. She was finding it difficult to even stretch her hands out from her sides, as muscles were becoming easily strained. How on earth to begin her rehabilitation if she couldn't use her limbs? I was at a loss to understand what was wrong, until one night I had a flash of insight: perhaps it was the anti-fungal medication? It had been prescribed for many months to come.

I undertook an online research, and discovered 'undocumented side-affects', anecdotally reported, of hair loss and muscle weakness from the medication. We took it up with Russell, her doctor, and he contacted the hospital physician who had prescribed the anti-fungal. It was agreed to cease the medication, and from that time forward, Julie regained her strength and her hair. It was a small thing looking back but at the time it was a tremendous liberation to have resolved that affliction.

For Julie to sustain her recovery path, it was vital she remain in touch with travelling. So, we undertook a trip to a workshop at Guthega in the Snowy Mountains in the first summer of the year she left the hospital, staying overnight at a camping ground in Mudgee, inland NSW. I was in trepidation about how she would handle climbing in and out of our camping bed in the back of the van, going to the amenities in the middle of the night, and psychologically overcoming the inevitable inconveniences. In fact, she handled the entire trip extremely well. Following the workshop, we drove south through Victoria and along the southern coast to Adelaide, where we excitedly watched a stage of the Tour Down Under cycling race. Then we travelled and camped through inland South Australia, across the red soil flatlands to Broken Hill in western NSW and, finally, home to Armidale. It was a fabulous success, and we both felt this was the opening of possibilities for Julie. Nonetheless, we had to choose easy camping conditions, but on the few occasions when we couldn't achieve that, she handled the difficulties well.

She continued to suffer from vertigo. We entered upon a long process of Eply technique sessions. With the help of Chris Walker, a local chiropractor who has studied brain injuries, we perfected the Eply technique and he identified her core-cerebellum condition, which is associated with eye movement. The Eply sessions reduced the degree of vertigo periods but Julie has continued to have these episodes, even four years later. This balance instability issue remains the most intransigent residue of the physical effects from her fall. The causes in the ear are easier to resolve than those in her cerebellum.

Critical events in my life, and thus also in Julie's, came up mid-2015, so we had to once again cancel our frequent flyer tickets for the summer bookings to India. Up until this time, Julie had been re-involved with her university work, which went some way towards reassurance in her post-fall identity process. To keep the 'fire burning', so to speak, we planned, and undertook in the van a big month-long camping trip to Tasmania. This trip was huge for Julie, to be able to sustain long periods of extended driving, new places and the risk of over-exhaustion setbacks from which she often can take up to a week to recover, or of falling over when dizziness strikes.

Despite extreme changes of weather, and Julie's growing hypersensitivity caused by processing so much change, combined with her having a cold, we managed to complete an interesting and successful adventure, with her concentrating intensely on every little move. This necessity, of her having to expend twice the energy as everyone else just to complete everyday tasks, is a condition that has continued up until this day.

We had planned the next summer of 2016 as the return to India, and booked the frequent flyer flights. But after our return from Tasmania, Julie tore the cartilage in her knee when swimming breaststroke. Unfortunately, it was a long time before we realised this was no ordinary muscular injury. In fact, it required surgery in Sydney. Julie was essentially disabled for most of the year, so we cancelled our plans for India once again.

We consoled ourselves by planning for the following summer of 2017 as the India-return venture, and booked accordingly. Feeling encouraged as the year progressed, we indulged in some, always enjoyable, itinerary research. As the months passed through winter, we came to realise it was a 'frighteningly' real possibility that the trip would happen. There were obstacles of a questionable cancer-burn sore on her shin with possible excision, all within a few weeks of leaving. And predictably, there was the immense number of tasks for house, garden and pets necessary to leave home for four months.

Despite a few question-marks above our heads, we poured energy into planning the trip and preparing for departure. It was an exhausting, mad rush to the point of departure and boarding the flight out of Armidale. That Julie was capable of sustaining her energy levels for the months of intense preparation activities, with this pending, unbelievable possibility that we might return to India, was extraordinary considering the last few years.

Julie was deeply anxious, and kept imagining all the rational problems, like the increase of multi-resistant bacteria in India, or the danger of having an accident from a moment of imbalance or indecision. We acknowledged these risks, and wove them into our plans, to expect the most relaxing and traffic-reduced itinerary, except for a few wild-cards. First of the wild-cards was Chennai, where we must fly in and remain a few days, to obtain the necessary communication services (and which were unsuccessful there) and also to see our 'adopted daughter' and

Julie's beloved nurse in hospital, Mythili. Chennai turned out to be an even more dementedly busy city than we'd remembered it, with little pedestrian comforts. Next, we were uncertain about our feelings in seeing the old British hill-station, Ooty, reportedly a shadow of its former charm (which turned out to be true).

In spite of the obstacles, Julie maintained a fairly comfortable mien, aside from some rainy days in Ooty, trapped indoors with a bad cold and chest condition, until the Christmas festival in Cochin began to pound her senses with the escalating noise and influx of North Indian tourists. After a delightful break in the spice-growing, elephant and tiger foothills of Kerala, we spent a conflicting month at familiar, beautiful Kovalam Beach near Trivandrum: re-meeting old friends, feeling aghast at the changes due to its increased growth, and attending the always wonderful Maharajah's Classical Indian music concerts in the palace grounds. Returning home via sparkling, orderly Singapore was a delight; we arrived back in Armidale with the usual sense of relief and disorientation following four months away.

This trip to India was an exceptional success for Julie's recovery. She returned to Australia with more self-confidence. It was not without considerable courage that she undertook such a potentially dangerous journey; she'd cried with nervousness in saying goodbye to her doctor, Russell, whom she had come to rely on. For us both, it completed another turn of the wheel in the process, which had been set in train that day in Trichy when we heard the electrical cracks outside our window.

Afterword (Julie)

May, 2018

Four years have passed since the accident in Trichy; we're back from another several months in India, though we're not quite grounded in Australia yet. Switching between these worlds is always bemusing. Of course, despite going back to India, there was no "returning full circle" to the time of four years ago; no retracing of footsteps, in reality. Surely, life is not meant to be reliving a past way of being, for then we human creatures would never change and grow. But I am grateful, happy, so fortunate, I know, to be reading Michael's words from my place in the sunshine and shadow, while remembering some of that past adventure of 2014.

I don't remember it all obviously, even from this account Michael has kept. 'The Fall' from Hotel Royal Sangam is (thankfully) a blank in my mind though I do, in a dream-like vision, see its beginnings: looking out from the window, the cable sparking and crackling near the ground below. Michael, though, endured consciously through the whole drama and fear of the long following moments and months, aware of the precarious state of my survival once in hospital in Trichy, bearing the complex nature of my physical, cerebral and resultant emotional conditions. As well, he had to manage the legal and practical issues of being in India and how (if ever) we'd return to Australia. He's had to bear with me ever since, and brain trauma creates complexity.

It was his plan to return to India eventually: despite my trepidation about that, he was right. Difficult though this most recent journey was at times, mainly due to my ongoing lack of balance, I'm sure it has recalibrated my brain, given me renewed inspiration, and amazement at the vagaries of life itself. What had this dramatic lacuna four years ago been all about, I've often wondered? It was a chasm in my life, then a reorientation, that is still unfolding. We all try to make interpretations of our life stories, don't we, as the road winds on. Yet two high points in that fateful year shine out as 'forever gifts' to me, as I think back now.

India, October, 2013

In Kasar Devi, in the lower hills of the Himalayan range, there is a much-revered small temple built upon a rocky cave, among pine trees, forested paths and wildflower grasses. It overlooks a vast open valley, the distance hemmed by the shining white line of high mountains, and the sacred peaks of Trishul and Nanda Devi. No-one was there in this silence at the temple except Michael and me; no human habitation to be seen but for scattered specks of cottages and a narrow road way below in the valley. A woodpecker tapped at a treetop. Michael had climbed a grassy path to the Shiva temple a little higher up, and I sat to wait on the flagstones, in an immense aloneness and sadness, flooded again by grief and loss from my mother's death a year ago. I wept without restraint, emptying my anguish into the endless space. But then! By my feet in a crack in the paving, I saw that a marigold seed had sown itself, and grown into the tiniest plant, with one miniscule orange flower glowing modestly. It was utter wonder! Comforted, made at peace by this miracle of life and its beauty, I no longer felt separate and alone, and never have, since. Emily Bronte wrote

"Though earth and man were gone
and suns and universes ceased to be,
And thou wert left alone,
Every existence would exist in thee.
There is not room for Death
Nor atom that his might could render void
Thou – thou art being and breath
And what thou art may never be destroyed."

This strength from the spaces of Kasar Devi lasted with me the rest of the long journey across India, through the beautiful and difficult scenarios that complex, amazing country always presents. Months later, I looked out from the lighthouse at Kovalam Beach and rejoiced in my feeling of wellness and happiness. Soon after, Michael and I left Kerala for Tamil Nadu, to the temples, history and artworks of Tanjore and Trichy, and met with the accident there.

Autumn, 2014.

After some months in hospital in India, Armidale and Sydney I returned to our home amongst the grazing land and ancient eucalyptus woods in the New England ranges of northern NSW. It is hushed and peaceful here too, though a working dog is barking across the valley, a magpie chortles, our little ancient Siamese cat, Sheena, is beside me as I lie under the yellow leaves looking up at endless blue sky. I am still weak but to me that doesn't matter as much as others impress that it should (I must exercise!). I am detached from the 'normalcy' of the world, at peace in some suspended space between life and death. I can watch the leaves, the sky, the birds flitting above, in timeless bliss. But I must find the energy to strive, to reconnect with human activity, to be functioning fully again, learning to walk without help, to cut a tomato, sweep the floor, to drive a car. I need to be as I once was, active and helpful and curious. This disconnected space of sky-gazing had been understood by dear Susan Elms, the therapist from the regional Brain Trauma unit, who had visited me in hospital, recognizing and explaining to us the symptoms of brain injury. Michael and I had felt so relieved when someone could spell out what was happening, and what needed to be done to relearn 'normality'. The 'peaceful bliss' aspect was fine but not the times of pain or bewilderment, the outbursts of emotion, the utter exhaustion of every small action, the pressure on Michael at my being so utterly dependent.

It was a privileged time apart, my at-home period of recovery. It was similar, a friend remarked, to the century-past practice of 'taking the waters' at spa towns of Europe, or malingering in a sanitorium. It was not as onerous as retreating to a Himalayan cave, yet still had the effect of reinforcing to me the maya of the world. "Abandon life and the world, so that you may know the life of the world" the Sufi poet Rumi had said. Perhaps this daydream space was illusion too, a result of the brain trauma; still, it remains clear in my memory, the never-ending recognition of some true knowledge we all share, like the sun sparkling on water.

www.ingramcontent.com/pod-product-compliance
Lightning Source LLC
Chambersburg PA
CBHW062220080426
42734CB00010B/1963